PSYCHOLOGY RESEARCH PROGRESS SERIES

SIGNIFICANCE OF INDIVIDUAL ASPIRATIONS IN HEALTH PSYCHOLOGY

PSYCHOLOGY RESEARCH PROGRESS SERIES

Jung Today: Volume 1 - Adulthood
Francesco Bisagni, Nadia Fina and Caterina Vezzoli (Editors)
2009. ISBN: 978-1-60741-893-1

Jung Today: Volume 2 - Childhood and Adolescence
Francesco Bisagni, Nadia Fina and Caterina Vezzoli (Editors)
2009. ISBN: 978-1-60741-894-8

Psychology Research Yearbook, Volume 1
Alexandra M. Columbus (Editor)
2009. ISBN: 978-1-60741-573-2

Suicide and the Creative Arts
Steven Stack and David Lester (Editors)
2009. ISBN: 978-1-60741-958-7

Suicide and the Creative Arts
Steven Stack and David Lester (Editors)
2009. ISBN: 978-1-60876-560-7 (Online Book)

Psychological Scientific Perspectives on Out of Body and Near Death Experiences
Craig D. Murray (Editor)
2009. ISBN: 978-1-60741-705-7

Psychological Scientific Perspectives on Out of Body and Near Death Experiences
Craig D. Murray (Editor)
2009. ISBN: 978-1-61668-241-5 (Online Book)

Psychology of Burnout: Predictors and Coping Mechanisms
Rachel V. Schwartzhoffer (Editor)
2009. ISBN: 978-1-60876-010-7

Perchance to Dream: The Frontiers of Dream Psychology
Stanley Krippner and Debbie Joffe Ellis (Editors)
2009. ISBN: 978-1-60876-123-4

Stress in the Year 2010 and Beyond
Michael F. Shaughnessy (Editor)
2009. ISBN: 978-1-60876-444-0

What Philosophers Say Compared with What Psychologists Find in Discerning Values: How Wise People Interpret Life
Dorothy Pushkar, Sheila Mason, Andrew Burr, Sarah Etezadi and Tracy Lyster
2010. ISBN: 978-1-60876-660-4

Neuropsychology of the Sense of Agency
Michela Balconi
2010. ISBN: 978-1-60876-358-0

The Psychological Impact of Living Under Violence and Poverty in Brazil
Giovanni Marcos Lovisi, Jair de Jesus Mari and Elie S. Valencia (Editors)
2010. ISBN: 978-1-60876-587-4

Sustainable Evidence-Based Decision-Making
Francesco Chiappelli
2010. ISBN: 978-1-60876-665-9

Children's Dreams
Barbara Szmigielska
2010. ISBN: 978-160876-704-5

A Multiple Self Theory of Personality
David Lester
2010. ISBN: 978-1-60876-783-0

Regulatory Fit and Persuasion Through Advocacy Messages and Narratives
Leigh Ann Vaughn
2010. ISBN: 978-1-60876-887-5

Environmental Psychology: New Developments
Jorge Valentín and Lucila Gamez (Editors)
2010. ISBN: 978-1-60876-911-7

Significance of Individual Aspirations in Health Psychology
Margitics Ferenc and Zsuzsa Pauwlik
2010. ISBN: 978-1-60876-124-1

PSYCHOLOGY RESEARCH PROGRESS SERIES

SIGNIFICANCE OF INDIVIDUAL ASPIRATIONS IN HEALTH PSYCHOLOGY

FERENC MARGITICS
AND
ZSUZSA PAUWLIK

Nova Science Publishers, Inc.
New York

LIBRARY OF CONGRESS CATALOGING-IN-PUBLICATION DATA

Ferenc, Margitics.
Significance of individual aspirations in health psychology / Margitics Ferenc and Zsuzsa Pauwlik.
p. cm.
Includes bibliographical references and index.
ISBN 978-1-60876-124-1 (hbk.)
1. Goal (Psychology) 2. Desire. 3. Values. 4. Well-being. 5. Depression, Mental. I. Pauwlik, Zsuzsa. II. Title.
BF505.G6F47 2009
153.8--dc22

2009028876

Published by Nova Science Publishers, Inc. † New York

CONTENTS

Preface		**ix**
Chapter 1	Correlation between Individual Aspirations and Subjective Well-Being	**1**
Chapter 2	Correlation between Individual Aspirations and Depression	**37**
Index		**59**

PREFACE

In our days, health psychology is based upon a dynamic approach to the personality. In this way, psychology does not primarily deal with the interrelation between the constant features of the personality and health, but interprets the human personality as a functional system, in which perceptions, cognitions, values, and personal ambitions constitute an organic whole, exerting their joint effects on health.

In view of all this, it is necessary to identify the personal goals, values, and aspirations that may serve as protective factors in preserving health, creating and maintaining psychic balance, and contributing to the elimination or counterbalancing of undesired behavior patterns. In this volume, the authors make an effort to find the answers to these questions. The authors examine the connections of personal aspirations with subjective well-being and certain symptoms of depression.

Chapter 1.—In the course of our research, we examined the level of subjective well-being among college students and what individual aspirations they had. There were 545 female and 167 male students (n=712) involved in the research. In terms of the indicators of subjective well-being, students scored the highest values in self-evaluation, followed by positive attitude toward life and pleasures of life. The lowest values measured on the depressive scale suggest the lack of depressive moods. No considerable difference between the two genders was measured in subjective well-being. The only exception to that was observed at somatic symptoms and reactions, as women were found to be more susceptible to such reactions than men. When examining the importance of individual aspirations, we recorded the highest points in health, personal progress, and social connections. Most participants in the survey found these personal aspirations very important. The college students involved in the project ascribed the lowest importance to the three extrinsic aspirations: fame, wealth, and image. Intrinsic aspirations were, therefore, favored by college students over the extrinsic ones. If priorities are examined in a breakdown according to genders, intrinsic aspirations were found more important by both sexes, with slight differences in emphasis. In terms of the probability of various types of aspirations, the highest scores were also measured in intrinsic aspirations. In that case, the order of priority was social relations, personal progress, and health. It was followed by social commitment and, finally, extrinsic aspirations, in the order of image, wealth, and fame. When the order of probability is examined in a breakdown according to genders, women fully comply with the general trend, whereas, in the case of the men, there is a slight deviation at one point only; they tend to place wealth before image. In terms of the implementation of the types of aspiration, the tendency is similar, as we find the highest points in the intrinsic ones, in the following order: social relations, health, and personal progress. Here, an extrinsic aspiration, image, wedged in, followed by social commitment, wealth, and fame. The order was the same in both genders. Individual aspirations— regardless of gender— were found to be in the closest correlation with a positive attitude towards life and self-esteem, explaining more than 33.2 % of the variance. Both of these indicators of subjective well-being were in the closest correlation with intrinsic aspirations, particularly with the likelihood and realization of personal advancement. In self-esteem, realized social commitment, and in a positive attitude towards, life the likelihood of establishing personal relations in the future were also present. Individual aspirations were found to be in the most remote correlation with Grob's disease existence indicators, amounting to 11.2% of the variance of somatic symptoms and complaints, and a mere 7.4% of the variance of personal problems. Somatic symptoms and complaints were in close interrelationship with the lack of health and realized social commitment, whereas personal problems were in a similar relationship with diminished chances of personal advancement, social commitment as an objective, and the realization of extrinsic aspirations.

Chapter 2.—The aim of our survey was to reveal the individual aspirations among college students, which may play an important role as protective factors in the preservation of mental health, particularly regarding sub-clinical depressive syndromes. There were 712 college students involved in the study (545 females and 167 males). The abridged version of Beck's Depression Inventory was used for the definition of the rate of depression, while the Aspiration Questionnaire was used to measure the rate of individual aspirations. In the course of estimating the importance of individual aspirations, we found intrinsic aspirations to be predominating in the case of college students for both genders, with a minor shifting of weight. While in the case of women, health, social relationships, and personal advancement were listed in this order of importance, in the case of men, personal advancement was listed in the first position, followed by the categories of health and social relationships. From among the symptoms of depression, social reservation was in the closest correlation with the importance of certain personal strivings, and within these, with the lack of intrinsic aspirations was highlighted. Certain symptoms of depression— regardless of generic affiliations— showed a very close correlation with the probability of nearly every personal aspiration, as well as with the realisation thereof; and within this, they were in a stronger correlation with the intrinsic aspirations than with those of extrinsic ones (in the case of men, there was a stronger correlation between the probability of every aspiration for depressive syndromes, and the realisation thereof were also found to be stronger than in the case of women). Examining the overall correlation among all three categories of individual aspirations (importance, probability, and realisation), in the case of depression, we found that depression showed a close negative correlation with the probability of personal growth and social relationships and the realisation of health, while a positive correlation was detected with the importance attributed to intrinsic aspirations, which explained almost one-fourth of the variances of depression altogether. The depressive syndromes found to be typical of college students (worthlessness, fatigue, hesitation, hopelessness, and dissatisfaction) showed a much closer correlation with the importance, probability, and realisation of individual aspirations in the case of men than in the case of women. From among the aforementioned symptoms of depression, individual aspirations had the closest correlation with hopelessness in the case of both genders. While in the case of men, the importance of intrinsic aspirations and the current dissatisfaction of these may lead principally to the development of hopelessness, for women, the development of the feeling of hopelessness is primarily correlated with an extrinsic aspiration, the importance of wealth, and the current lack thereof. In the case of the rest of depressive syndromes, the explanatory power of the correlation with individual aspirations was different for women and men.

Chapter 1

CORRELATION BETWEEN INDIVIDUAL ASPIRATIONS AND SUBJECTIVE WELL-BEING

ABSTRACT

In the course of our research, we examined the level of subjective well-being among college students and what individual aspirations they had. There were 545 male and 167 male students (n=712) involved in the research. In terms of the indicators of subjective well-being, students scored the highest values in self-evaluation, followed by positive attitude toward life, and pleasures of life. The low values measured on the depressive scale suggest a lack of depressive moods. No considerable difference between the two genders was measured in subjective well-being. The only exemption to that was observed in somatic symptoms and reactions, as women were found to be more susceptible to such reactions than men. When examining the importance of individual aspirations, we recorded the highest points in health, personal progress, and social connections. Most participants in the survey found these personal aspirations very important. The college students involved in the project ascribed the lowest importance to the three extrinsic aspirations: fame, wealth, and image. Intrinsic aspirations were, therefore, favored by college students over the extrinsic ones. If priorities are examined in a breakdown according to genders, intrinsic aspirations were found more important by both sexes, with slight differences in emphasis. In terms of the probability of various types of aspirations, the highest scores were also measured in intrinsic aspirations. In that case, the order of priority was social relations, personal progress, and health. It was followed by social commitment and, finally, extrinsic aspirations, in the order of image, wealth, and fame. When the order of probability is examined in a breakdown according to genders, women fully comply with the general trend, whereas in the case of the men, there is a slight deviation at one point only; they tend to place wealth before image. In terms of the implementation of the types of aspiration, the tendency is similar, as we find the highest points in the intrinsic ones, in the following order: social relations, health, and personal progress. Here, an extrinsic aspiration, image, wedged in, followed by social commitment, wealth, and fame. The order was the same in both genders. Individual aspirations—regardless of gender—were found to be in the closest correlation with a positive attitude towards life and self-esteem, explaining more than 33.2% of the variance. Both of these indicators of subjective well-being were in the closest correlation with intrinsic aspirations, particularly with the likelihood and realization of personal advancement. In self-esteem, realized social commitment, and a positive attitude towards life, the likelihood of establishing personal relations in the future were also present. Individual aspirations were found to be in the most remote correlation with Grob's disease existence indicators, amounting to 11.2% of the variance of somatic symptoms and complaints, and a mere 7.4% of the variance of personal problems. Somatic symptoms and complaints were in close interrelationship with the lack of health and realized social commitment, whereas personal problems were in similar relationship with diminished chances of personal advancement, social commitment as an objective, and the realization of extrinsic aspirations.

1. Introduction

1.1. Individual Aspirations and Subjective Well-Being

The concept of subjective well-being is extremely complex, and the approaches various experts use are also varied. Diener arranges the recent approaches into three groups [1]:

- The first type of theories contains those that follow the footsteps of antique thinkers and philosophers and regard subjective well-being as the possession of positive characteristic features and/or emotions that are based upon the fulfillment and activation of personal ambitions and will lead to self-expression and self-implementation.
- The second category contains the so-called top-down models, emphasizing the role of personality and the interpretation of life experience in the definition of subjective well-being. In these theories,

subjective well-being is identified with satisfaction with life, which is based upon subjective value judgments and is closely related to the evaluative and attributive functions of the personality.

- The third group of theories is the one that includes the subjective, bottom-up approaches. These theories consider subjective well-being as the summary of pleasure experienced by the person concerned. An individual is happy after, and as a result of, gathering a large number of positive emotions, moods, and happy moments.

Today, it is obvious that it is necessary to integrate the various theories, as any one of the approaches above in itself will not be suitable for the interpretation of the complex issue of subjective well-being.

According to recent research, it is possible to describe subjective well-being with three major factors [1]:

- A level of satisfaction with life as a whole, referring to a cognitive judgment system, with which the individual evaluates his/her life in an overall way.
- Frequency and intensity of positive emotions/affectivity—pleasure and happiness.
- The relative scarcity of negative emotions, depression, fear, anxiety, sadness, and other negative situations.

The fact that the individual factors—pleasant emotions, satisfaction with life, negative emotions—are separate and independent of each other, has been justified by several surveys [2].

Although formerly it was believed that positive and negative emotions were located on the opposing ends of the same axis, today, it is regarded as proven that the levels of positive and negative emotions within one individual are relatively independent of each other. There is evidence suggesting that separate neurological operations are responsible for pleasant and unpleasant emotions [3].

Diener [3] asserts that subjective well-being has several clearly discernible components: satisfaction with life; satisfaction with various parts with life, e.g., job, marriage; the high levels of positive emotions (pleasant experiences and moods); and the low level of negative emotions (unpleasant experiences and moods).

Initial research projects into subjective well-being examined the connections between the personality and happiness, seeking an answer to

The Hungarian version of the scale was successfully used by Martos et al. [15] in their research program. They found the reliability of the scale excellent (Cronbach-alpha=0.890).

Hungarian Version of the Bern Subjective Well-Being Inventory [16]

Grob [17] describes two dimensions of subjective well-being: satisfaction and "disease existence." The four components of satisfaction are: a positive attitude to life, a positive self-esteem, the lack of depressive mood, and pleasures in life. Positive attitude towards life means, on the one hand, that the individual has a generally positive approach to life and, on the other hand, that the person is convinced that he or she lives a meaningful life. Depressive mood means the lack of energy, sadness, and withdrawal. The lack of depressive mood is an important indicator of subjective well-being, of satisfaction with life. Pleasures in life mean a positive evaluation and appreciation of human existence, as well as the acceptance of one's personal abilities and characteristics. The two components of "disease existence" are personal problems, on the one hand, and the somatic symptoms and reactions on the other. Personal problems include to what extent a person is preoccupied and annoyed by various problems. Personal problems also include how the individual recognizes and accept the problems that crop up in their direct social environment, as well as how sensitive the individual is to the problematic situations. Somatic symptoms and reactions mean the ability of the individual to convert his or her inner tensions into somatic symptoms.

The questionnaire developed by Grob contains the following dimensions:

- A positive attitude towards life
- Personal problems
- Somatic symptoms and reactions
- Self-esteem
- Depressive mood
- Pleasure in life

Respondents are requested to mark on a seven-grade Likert scale to what extent a statement applies to them.

The Hungarian adaptation of the questionnaire was done by Sallay [17], who found the reliability of the scales was good (Cronbach-alpha=0.69-0.81).

subjective well-being is identified with satisfaction with life, which is based upon subjective value judgments and is closely related to the evaluative and attributive functions of the personality.

- The third group of theories is the one that includes the subjective, bottom-up approaches. These theories consider subjective well-being as the summary of pleasure experienced by the person concerned. An individual is happy after, and as a result of, gathering a large number of positive emotions, moods, and happy moments.

Today, it is obvious that it is necessary to integrate the various theories, as any one of the approaches above in itself will not be suitable for the interpretation of the complex issue of subjective well-being.

According to recent research, it is possible to describe subjective well-being with three major factors [1]:

- A level of satisfaction with life as a whole, referring to a cognitive judgment system, with which the individual evaluates his/her life in an overall way.
- Frequency and intensity of positive emotions/affectivity—pleasure and happiness.
- The relative scarcity of negative emotions, depression, fear, anxiety, sadness, and other negative situations.

The fact that the individual factors—pleasant emotions, satisfaction with life, negative emotions—are separate and independent of each other, has been justified by several surveys [2].

Although formerly it was believed that positive and negative emotions were located on the opposing ends of the same axis, today, it is regarded as proven that the levels of positive and negative emotions within one individual are relatively independent of each other. There is evidence suggesting that separate neurological operations are responsible for pleasant and unpleasant emotions [3].

Diener [3] asserts that subjective well-being has several clearly discernible components: satisfaction with life; satisfaction with various parts with life, e.g., job, marriage; the high levels of positive emotions (pleasant experiences and moods); and the low level of negative emotions (unpleasant experiences and moods).

Initial research projects into subjective well-being examined the connections between the personality and happiness, seeking an answer to questions as to whether long-lasting happiness as a feature of the personality exists or whether there are personal characteristic features that are closely related to happiness. Several research programs suggest that certain characteristic features, such as extraversion, show a positive correlation with well-being [4], whereas neuroticism has a negative effect on personal happiness [5]. Personal characteristic features, however, only explain approximately 30% of the variance [6], so the question is still open as to what other specific factors are responsible for subjective well-being.

New tendencies in psychology, emerging in the late eighties and early nineties, offered new possibilities for measuring subjective well-being and subjective satisfaction with life. The new psychological approaches tend to place more emphasis on personal endeavors [7], personal objectives [8], and individual aspirations and strivings [9, 10].

These new research trends draw inspiration from the work of humanistic theoreticians like Rogers, Maslow, and Fromm, who believe that our decisions regarding important things in life, what we do in order to achieve our objectives, and how we utilize our internal potentials are the decisive factors in our personal subjective well-being. We believe that our life is sensible and valuable if and when our objectives are congruent with our internal selves, and we are committed to reach our goals, thus improving our personalities.

In Emmons's theory [7], personality is interpreted as a motivation system, in which the emphasis is on the personal objectives (or system of objectives) that drive human behavior and on the achievement of the objectives.

The research conducted by Emmons and Diener [11] suggest that individuals who regard their own actions as ones that do not generate conflicts tend to be more satisfied with life. In another examination intended to study the interrelations of personal goals, social and internal resources, and well-being/satisfaction with life, Diener and Fujita [12] found that social and internal resources have a considerable effect on satisfaction with life. Non-social external resources (e.g., material goods, money) do not appear to influence emotional well-being, but they correlate with satisfaction with life to a medium extent. Furthermore, an examination of the individual patterns of various resources revealed differences between men and women. Women find social objectives, such as emotional control and social skills, including the resources required for achieving these goals, more important than men do. The system of objectives of men, on the other hand, largely contains performance objectives like authority, achievements in sports, and knowledge acquired through experience. The resources leading to these goals are primarily performance and instrumental means.

Kasser and Ryan [9], when examining the connections among values, objectives, and subjective well-being, found that individuals giving priority to extrinsic goals (their endeavors are focused on financial success and the acquisition of material goods) demonstrated a generally lower well-being and a worse psychological situation, regardless of their gender, than those for whom intrinsic goals (self-acceptance, social relations, and social commitments) were more important.

The research programs conducted by Kasser and Ryan [10], as well as other researchers, among people of various age and social backgrounds (lower, middle, and upper classes) in cultures different from that of the U.S., suggest that there is a reverse proportion between the attribution of great importance to material values and subjective well-being. The studies mentioned above justify the theories of humanistic thinkers that for subjective well-being, intrinsic objectives are more central than extrinsic ones.

Personal strivings, as dynamic characteristics of the personality, may function as important indicators of subjective well-being. In the course of our research, we intended to reveal the level of subjective well-being of college students, what individual aspirations they had, and what connections existed between individual aspirations and subjective well-being. We also intended to find any differences, if such existed, between the two genders in this respect.

1.2. Research Hypotheses

Our initial research hypotheses were the following:

1. There are no differences in the levels of subjective well-being between the two genders [2, 13].
2. For college students (in accordance with the representative samples from Hungary), intrinsic objectives, particularly health, personal advancement, and social relations are the most important [14].
3. In terms of personal aspirations, there will considerable differences between the two genders, with women attributing greater significance to the intrinsic aspirations and image and men regarding wealth more important [14].
4. As for intrinsic aspirations, women will find health and social relations the most important, while men tend to ascribe the greatest importance to personal advancement [14].

5. Intrinsic goals tend to increase, whereas the extrinsic ones reduce, the level of subjective well-being [9].
6. Out of the components of subjective well-being, it is satisfaction with life with which the realization and likelihood of both the intrinsic and extrinsic aspirations are in a positive correlation [13].
7. All the three levels of individual aspirations (importance, likelihood, and realization) are in close correlation with certain indicators of subjective well-being.

2. METHOD

2.1. Participants

Data was collected among students at the College of Nyíregyháza. We collected data randomly at every faculty, and participation was voluntary and done with their consent. There were 750 students who took part in the research, and 712 of them provided valuable data (545 women and 167 men).

The average age was 19.98 (standard deviation, 1.58) and the median value was 20 years.

The test groups were organized according the results the participants scored on the inventories measuring subjective well-being, arranging the students into four quarters of the sample (Chart 1).

Chart 1. The quartiles of scores on aggregate chart scales of subjective well-being

	Quartiles	
	first	third
Diener's Satisfaction with Life Scale	17	27
Bern Subjective Well-Being Questionnaire: Positive attitude towards life	25	31
Bern Subjective Well-Being Questionnaire: Personal problems	18	26
Bern Subjective Well-Being Questionnaire: Somatic symptoms and reactions	13	21
Bern Subjective Well-Being Questionnaire: Self-esteem	15	20
Bern Subjective Well-Being Questionnaire: Depressive mood	8	13
Bern Subjective Well-Being Questionnaire: Pleasure of life	15	20

Students scoring low on the scale were arranged into the first quarter of the sample, whereas students scoring the highest on the scale were placed in the fourth quarter.

Upon examination of the Diener's Satisfaction with Life Scale, 178 students were in the group representing the lowest scores, and 184 students belonged to the group with the highest scores.

Upon examination of the positive attitude towards life, 176 students were in the group representing the lowest scores, and 184 students belonged to the group with the highest scores.

Upon examination of the personal problems, 179 students were in the group representing the lowest scores, and 171 students belonged to the group with the highest scores.

Upon examination of the somatic symptoms and reactions, 174 students were in the group representing the lowest scores, and 188 students belonged to the group with the highest scores.

Upon examination of self-esteem, 175 students were in the group representing the lowest scores, and 181 students belonged to the group with the highest scores.

Upon examination of depressive mood, 186 students were in the group representing the lowest scores, and 174 students belonged to the group with the highest scores

Upon examination of the pleasure of life, 174 students were in the group representing the lowest scores, and 187 students belonged to the group with the highest scores.

2.2. Measures

2.2.1. Examination of Subjective Well-Being

Hungarian Version of the Diener's Life Satisfaction Scale [3]

Diener [3] asserts that subjective well-being is an indicator of how individuals evaluate their lives from cognitive and affective aspects. Individuals make judgments about their lives as a whole and about various parts of the whole, e.g., work, family, marriage, etc. In this way, subjective well-being has several components independent of each other. The scale measures the cognitive factor and global satisfaction with live with the help of five statements. Respondents marked the validity of the statements for their particular life on a seven-grade Likert-scale.

The Hungarian version of the scale was successfully used by Martos et al. [15] in their research program. They found the reliability of the scale excellent (Cronbach-alpha=0.890).

Hungarian Version of the Bern Subjective Well-Being Inventory [16]

Grob [17] describes two dimensions of subjective well-being: satisfaction and "disease existence." The four components of satisfaction are: a positive attitude to life, a positive self-esteem, the lack of depressive mood, and pleasures in life. Positive attitude towards life means, on the one hand, that the individual has a generally positive approach to life and, on the other hand, that the person is convinced that he or she lives a meaningful life. Depressive mood means the lack of energy, sadness, and withdrawal. The lack of depressive mood is an important indicator of subjective well-being, of satisfaction with life. Pleasures in life mean a positive evaluation and appreciation of human existence, as well as the acceptance of one's personal abilities and characteristics. The two components of "disease existence" are personal problems, on the one hand, and the somatic symptoms and reactions on the other. Personal problems include to what extent a person is preoccupied and annoyed by various problems. Personal problems also include how the individual recognizes and accept the problems that crop up in their direct social environment, as well as how sensitive the individual is to the problematic situations. Somatic symptoms and reactions mean the ability of the individual to convert his or her inner tensions into somatic symptoms.

The questionnaire developed by Grob contains the following dimensions:

- A positive attitude towards life
- Personal problems
- Somatic symptoms and reactions
- Self-esteem
- Depressive mood
- Pleasure in life

Respondents are requested to mark on a seven-grade Likert scale to what extent a statement applies to them.

The Hungarian adaptation of the questionnaire was done by Sallay [17], who found the reliability of the scales was good (Cronbach-alpha=0.69-0.81).

2.2.2. Survey of the Individual Aspirations

Hungarian Version of the Aspiration Inventory [11]

The self-determination theory of Deci and Ryan [18, 19] constitutes the theoretical foundation of the questionnaire, according to which the sound functioning, growth and inner integration of a personality, is primarily driven by the efforts to satisfy certain innate and universal needs. The authors identify three of these needs as elementary: the individual's desire for autonomy, the individual's desire for positive relations, and an ability for competent, independent action. These basic needs serve as the major motivational forces of the personality. It is possible to satisfy these needs through self-motivation (intrinsic motives) and external motivation (extrinsic motives). The authors revealed the most characteristic intrinsic and extrinsic motives through empirical research. The motives were formulated in the form of aspirations, or objectives in life.

The Aspiration Inventory [10] is a means of revealing long-term objectives and aspirations; it contains a total of 35 aspirations (objective, motive), clustered around seven categories of goals in life, represented by the seven scales of the questionnaire. Five items belong to each of the seven scales. These are the following:

- Wealth
- Reputation
- Image (good appearance)
- Growth (personal advancement)
- Social relations (good personal connections)
- Society (social commitment)
- Health

Respondents are supposed to judge the aspirations listed in the questionnaire according to three aspects on a seven-grade Likert-scale:

- Importance (How important is the objective concerned for you?)
- Probability (What is the likelihood of this happening to you in the future?)
- Realization (How much of the objective above have you been able to achieve?)

The most important extrinsic motivations (aspirations) are: wealth, reputation, and image. The primary intrinsic motivations (aspirations) are: personal advancement, social relations, and social commitment. Kasser and Ryan [10] assert that health does not clearly belong to any of the aspirations. In compliance with the findings of several international research programs, V. Komlósi et al. [14], as a result of a survey in Hungary, listed health with the intrinsic aspirations.

In the course of the Hungarian adaptation of the questionnaire, V. Komlósi et al. [14] found the reliability of the dimensions are excellent (Cronbach-alpha=0.72-0.91).

3. RESULTS

3.1. Descriptive and Comparative Statistics

The descriptive and comparative statistics of the findings achieved with Diener's Life Satisfaction Scale and the Bern Subjective Well-being Inventory are provided (for the whole of the sample and in a breakdown according to the two genders) in Chart 2. In order to make the figures comparative, the average values and dispersions are set to one answer on the scale.

When examining university students' satisfaction with life, Diener et al. [2] measured an average of 4.7 (dispersion=1.28). In our college students, we found a value somewhat lower than that; our findings approximately match a medium value on Likert's scale.

Out of Grob's satisfaction index, students scored the highest values at self-esteem, followed by positive attitude towards life and pleasures of life, with almost the same figures. The low scores on the scale of depressive mood is an indicator of the lack of depressive mood.

The indicators of Grob's "disease existence" were low, with the indicators of personal problems somewhat higher than those of somatic reactions. These values—as matched to Likert's five-grade scale—suggest a high level of self-esteem, a somewhat above-average level of the positive attitude toward life and pleasures of life, an average level of personal problems, and levels below the average at somatic symptoms and depressive mood. Sallay [17] conducted a survey among adolescents and found similar values, except at self-esteem (average=1.96, dispersion=0.67), where their figure was lower and at depressive mood (average=3.68, dispersion=0.71), where their figure was higher. These differences are explained by the changes of the adolescent age, and in the sample we examined were not characterized by these deviations.

Chart 2. The descriptive and comparative statistics of Diener's Life Satisfaction Scale and the Bern Subjective Well-being Inventory

	Total (n=712)		Women (n=545)		Men (n=167)	
	Mean Value	Standard Deviation	Mean Value	Standard Deviation	Mean Value	Standard Deviation
Diener's Satisfaction with Life Scale	4.38	1.22	4.40	1.20	4.34	1.28
Bern Subjective Well-Being Questionnaire: Positive attitude towards life	3.46	0.65	3.46	0.64	3.47	0.67
Bern Subjective Well-Being Questionnaire: Personal problems	2.75	0.85	2.77	0.9	2.67	0.70
Bern Subjective Well-Being Questionnaire: Somatic symptoms and reactions	2.15***	0.75	2.21	0.75	1.96	0.71
Bern Subjective Well-Being Questionnaire: Self-esteem	4.45	0.87	4.45	0.85	4.47	0.92
Bern Subjective Well-Being Questionnaire: Depressive mood	2.16	0.70	2.14	0.68	2.24	0.74
Bern Subjective Well-Being Questionnaire: Pleasure of life	3.46	0.66	3.46	0.64	3.42	0.74

*$p<0.05$; **$p<0.01$; ***$p<0.001$.

A comparative statistical analysis of the two genders shows any considerable difference between men and women at the somatic symptoms and reactions only. Women appear to be more susceptible to such reactions than men (t=3.944, p<0.005).

Chart 3. The descriptive and comparative statistics of Aspiration Inventory

	Total (n=712)		Women (n=545)		Men (n=167)	
	Mean Value	Standard Deviation	Mean Value	Mean Value	Standard Deviation	Mean Value
Wealth: importance	22.8	5.6	23.6	5.7	24.1	5.4
Wealth: probability	19.9	5.1	19.8	5	20.3	5.5
Wealth: realization	15.1	5.5	15	5.4	15.2	5.9
Reputation: importance	17**	7.3	16.6	7.2	18.4	7.4
Reputation: probability	14.9***	5.9	14.5	5.7	16.4	6.3
Reputation: realization	11.5***	5	11.1	4.7	12.9	5.7
Image: importance	23***	6.7	23.8	6.6	20.6	6.7
Image: probability	21.1***	5.9	21.7	5.8	19.3	6.1
Image: realization	19.4*	6.3	19.7	6.2	18.3	6.5
Personal advancement: importance	32.3	13.2	32.1	8.4	32.6	22.8
Personal advancement: probability	26.8*	4.7	27.1	4.5	26	5
Personal advancement: realization	21.8	5.5	22	5.5	21.1	5.6
Personal relationships: importance	32***	3.2	32.3	2.8	30.1	4.4
Personal relationships: probability	28.5***	4.7	29	4.2	26.8	5.8
Personal relationships: realization	24.5***	9.4	25.7	9.4	22.6	7.2
Social commitment: importance	25.6*	5.8	25.9	5.6	24.5	6.4
Social commitment: probability	22.3**	5.7	22.7	5.6	21	5.9
Social commitment: realization	16.7	6.1	17	6	16.1	6.1
Health: importance	32.3***	3.4	32.7	2.9	31	4.5
Health: probability	26.1***	5.5	26.6	5.3	24.5	6.1
Health: realization	23.5*	6.5	23.8	6.4	22.4	6.8
Intrinsic: importance	121.5***	11.7	122.8	10.3	117.3	14.8
Intrinsic: probability	103.7***	16.1	105.2	14.9	98.8	18.6
Intrinsic: realization	86.9**	19.7	88.1	19.2	82.9	20.1
Extrinsic: importance	64.7	17.1	64.6	17.2	65.1	16.9
Extrinsic: probability	56.6	14.2	56.6	14	56.4	14.8
Extrinsic: realization	46.2	14.2	46.1	13.8	46.7	15.5

*p<0.05; **p<0.01; ***p<0.001.

The descriptive and comparative statistics of Aspiration Inventory are summarized in Chart 3.

In the whole sample, when the importance of the various aspirations was examined, the highest values were measured at health, personal advancement, and social relations. Most respondents found these aspirations extremely important, which is also indicated by the fact that the dispersion was the smallest at health and social relations (the large standard deviation found at personal growth, on the other hand, indicates the large personal differences at this point). The least important goals in life for the respondents were the three extrinsic aspirations, reputation, wealth and image. Intrinsic aspirations are, therefore, favored by college students over the extrinsic ones. These findings largely coincide with the results obtained by V. Komlósi et al. [14] as a result of their examination conducted on a representative sample (with the exception of the value of standard deviation found at personal growth, which was larger at their sample). Szondy [13] also found intrinsic aspirations more characteristic in his sample of late adolescent age (average age: 17.38 years). The order of importance of the aspirations was the following: social relations, health, and personal growth, followed by social responsibility. The adolescents also listed extrinsic aspirations with the least important ones in the order of wealth, image, and, finally, reputation.

If we examine the order of importance, we find the intrinsic aspirations on the top of the lists in both genders, with smaller shifts in emphasis. While the order of importance for women is health, social relations, and personal advancement, men place personal advancement to the first position, followed by health and social relations. Social commitment is the fourth in the list of both genders. On the list of women, it is followed by image and wealth, with approximately the same values, whereas wealth precedes image on the list of men. Reputation is the last on the lists of both sexes. Our findings, in connection with the extrinsic aspirations, match those of V. Komlósi et al. [14], obtained from their survey of a representative sample. They found health as the most important intrinsic aspiration in both genders, followed by social relations on the list of women and personal growth on the list of men. The comparative statistical analysis (two-paired t-test) suggests that women scored considerably higher at the combined index of intrinsic aspirations, health, social relations, image, and social commitment. Men, on the other hand, gave higher points to reputation. Szondy [13] also observed this difference between the two sexes, except in the higher value of reputation on the list of men. No considerable difference was observed between the two genders at the combined index of extrinsic aspirations, personal growth, and wealth. These findings only partially match the results obtained by V. Komlósi et al. [14] from their representative sample. In their findings, men scored significantly higher in their aspirations for wealth, whereas women scored considerably higher in image, personal advancement, social relations, social commitment, and health than men did.

An examination of the entire sample from the aspect of the probability of the various aspirations revealed the highest values were also measured at the intrinsic aspirations, in the order of social relations, personal advancement, and health. They are followed by the extrinsic aspirations, in the order of the image, wealth, and reputation. Szondy [13] found the same order in late adolescent age. In an examination of the order or probability according to the two genders, we find the same tendency in women. In men, there is only one deviation, as they place wealth before image. In the probability of various aspirations, we found similar differences to those observed in the degree of importance. The only exception was that women gave considerably greater emphasis to personal advancement.

When analyzing the realization of the aspirations in the whole sample, the highest values are observed in the intrinsic aspirations. The order is the following: social relations, health, and personal growth. The fourth one here is an extrinsic aspiration—image —followed by social commitment, wealth, and reputation. This was the order in both genders. In connection with realization, Szondy [13] found a similar pattern among adolescents, with slight changes of emphasis: health, social relations, personal advancement, image, social responsibility, wealth, and reputation. In the probability of various aspirations, we found similar differences to those observed at the degree of importance. The only exception to that was that no significant difference between the two genders was observable in terms of the realization of social commitment.

Unfortunately, we did not have an opportunity to compare the probability and realization of the various aspirations with the representative sample, as V. Komlósi et al. [14] did not provide relevant data in their study.

3.2. Differences in Individual Aspirations Relative to Different Levels of Subjective Well-Being

It has also been examined whether there were any differences in terms of personal aspirations between the two groups created according to the results the individuals scored on Diener's Life Satisfaction Scale and the Bernese Subjective Well-Being Inventory. Those who scored low on these scales belonged to the first quarter, and those who scored high were in the fourth quarter.

Figure 1 contains the average values of the scales, showing the significant differences in the personal aspirations between the two groups created according to their scores achieved on Diener's Life Satisfaction Scale.

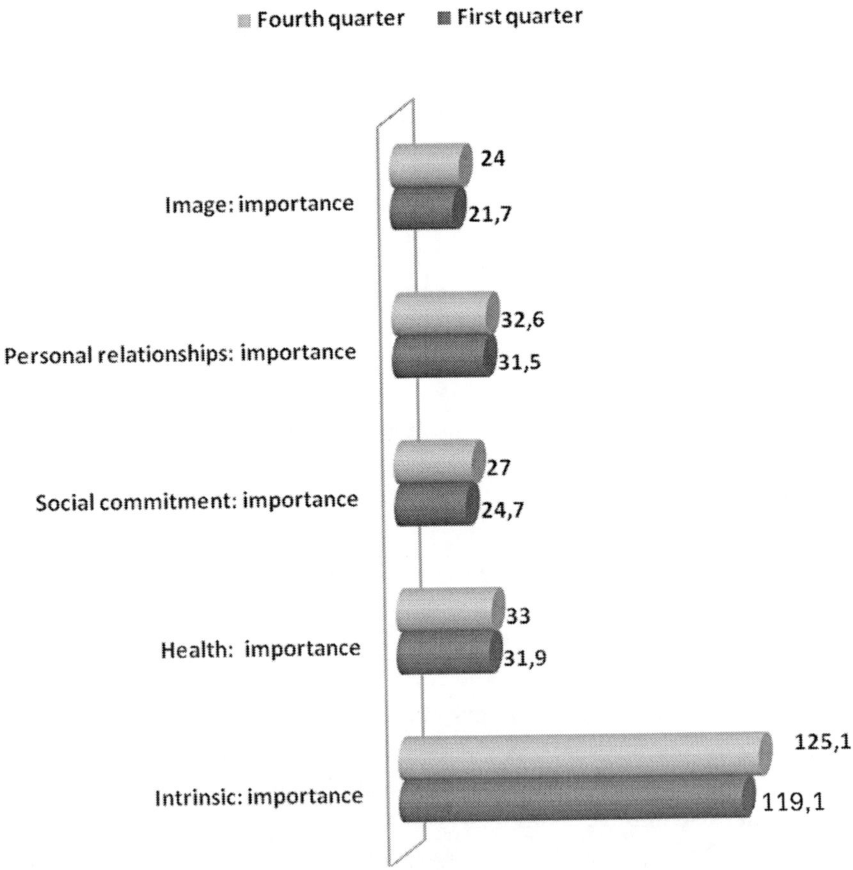

Figure 1. The average values of the scales showing the significant differences in the personal aspirations between the two groups created according to their scores achieved on Diener's Life Satisfaction Scale.

According to the comparative statistical examination (two-sample t-test), the students achieving higher values (in quarter four) in personal aspirations were characterized by a considerably higher level of intrinsic aspirations. Within that ($t=5.044$, $p<0.000$), social responsibility ($t=3.196$, $p<0.000$), establishing social relations ($t=3.186$, $p<0.002$), and a healthy way of life (t=3.063, p<0.003), out of extrinsic aspirations, they attributed more significance to improving their image and good external appearance than students with a lower level of life satisfaction did.

Considerable differences have been found in the attitudes toward personal aspirations between the test groups created according to the results achieved on Grob's Satisfaction Scales (positive attitude to life, self-esteem, and pleasure of life) (Figure 2).

Out of the categories of personal aspirations, pleasure of life showed the largest difference between the two groups. The individuals appreciating the pleasure of life attributed considerably more significance to all intrinsic aspirations (intrinsic aspirations: t=4.921, p<0.000; personal advancement: t=5.333, p<0.000; personal relationships: t=4.248, p<0.000; social commitment: t=2.941, p<0.003; and health: t=2.892, p<0.004), and all the extrinsic aspirations, with the exception of wealth (extrinsic aspirations: t=2.629, p<0.009; image: t=2.979, p<0.003; and reputation: t=2.517, p<0.012), than those who do not have such a positive attitude toward life.

The individuals appreciating the pleasure of life attributed considerably more significance to all intrinsic aspirations (intrinsic aspirations: t=4.766, p<0.000), and within that, social relations (t=3.241, p<0.001), healthy way of life (t=3.331, p<0.001), and social responsibility (t=2.345, p<0.019). As for extrinsic aspirations, they find fame more important (t=2.574, p<0.013) than people with a less positive attitude toward life do.

Individuals with a higher self-esteem found all the elements of intrinsic aspirations more important than people with a lower self-esteem (intrinsic aspirations: t=4.504, p<0.000; personal advancement: t=6.685, p<0.000; personal relationships: t=3.278, p<0.001; health: t=4,.504, p<0.004; social commitment: t=2.373, p<0.018).

Figure 3 contains the averages of the significant differences observed in the personal aspirations of the test groups created according to their results achieved on the depressive mood scale of Grob's satisfaction indicators.

Individuals not characterized by a depressive mood found intrinsic aspirations (intrinsic aspirations: t=4.461, p<0.000), especially social relations (t=3.777, p<0.000) and a healthy way of life (t=3.505, p<0.001), a lot more important, than people with a depressive mood. They, on the other hand, attributed more significance to becoming rich than those without a depressive mood did (t=2.983, p<0.003).

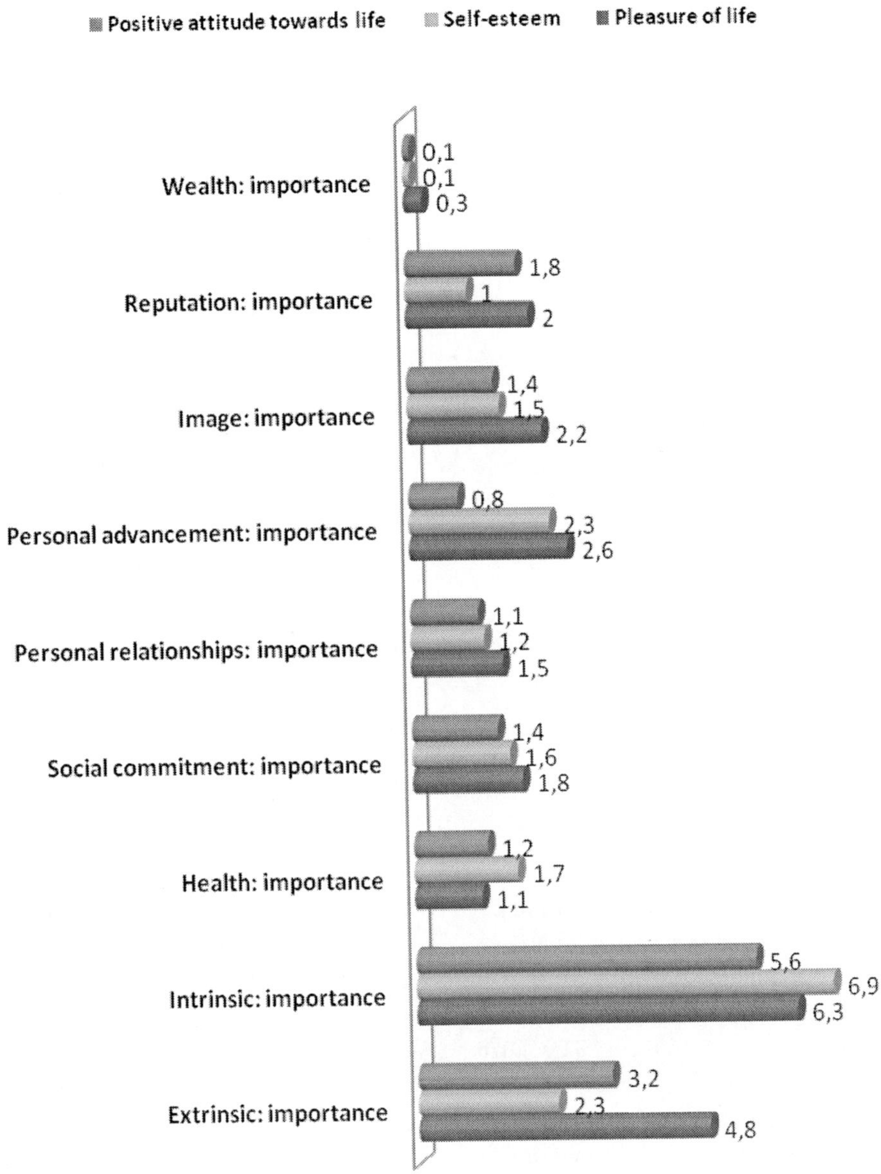

Figure 2. Differences in individual aspirations between the test groups arranged according to the results achieved on Grob's Satisfaction Inventory (positive attitude towards life, self-esteem, pleasure of life), from the aspect of the group that scored high on the scale (fourth quarter).

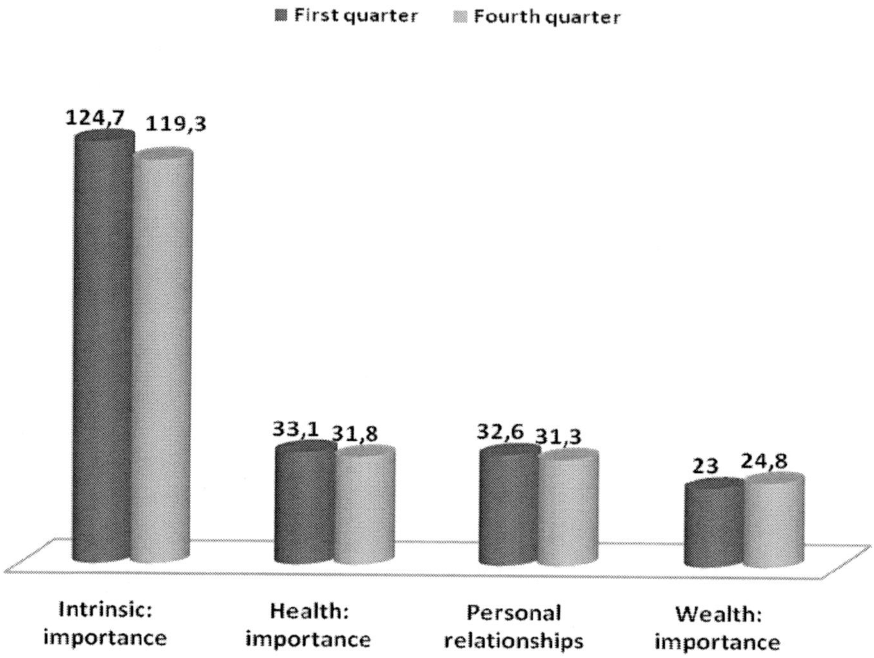

Figure 3. The averages of the significant differences observed in the personal aspirations in the test groups created according to their results achieved on the depressive mood scale of Grob's satisfaction indicators.

Figure 4 contains the averages of the significant differences in personal aspirations between the test groups created according to their results achieved on the scales of personal problems and somatic symptoms and complaints of Grob's "disease existence" scale.

Participants suffering from a higher number of personal problems found extrinsic aspirations ($t=2.010$, $p<0.045$) more important, especially, becoming rich ($t=2.244$, $p<0.025$). The intrinsic aspiration they found important was social responsibility ($t=2.304$, $p<0.0022$) —it was more important for them than for people with fewer personal problems.

People with somatic symptoms ascribed much more importance to social responsibility ($t=3.273$, $p<0.001$), and much less to a healthy lifestyle ($t=2.040$, $p<0.042$), than participants with fewer somatic symptoms.

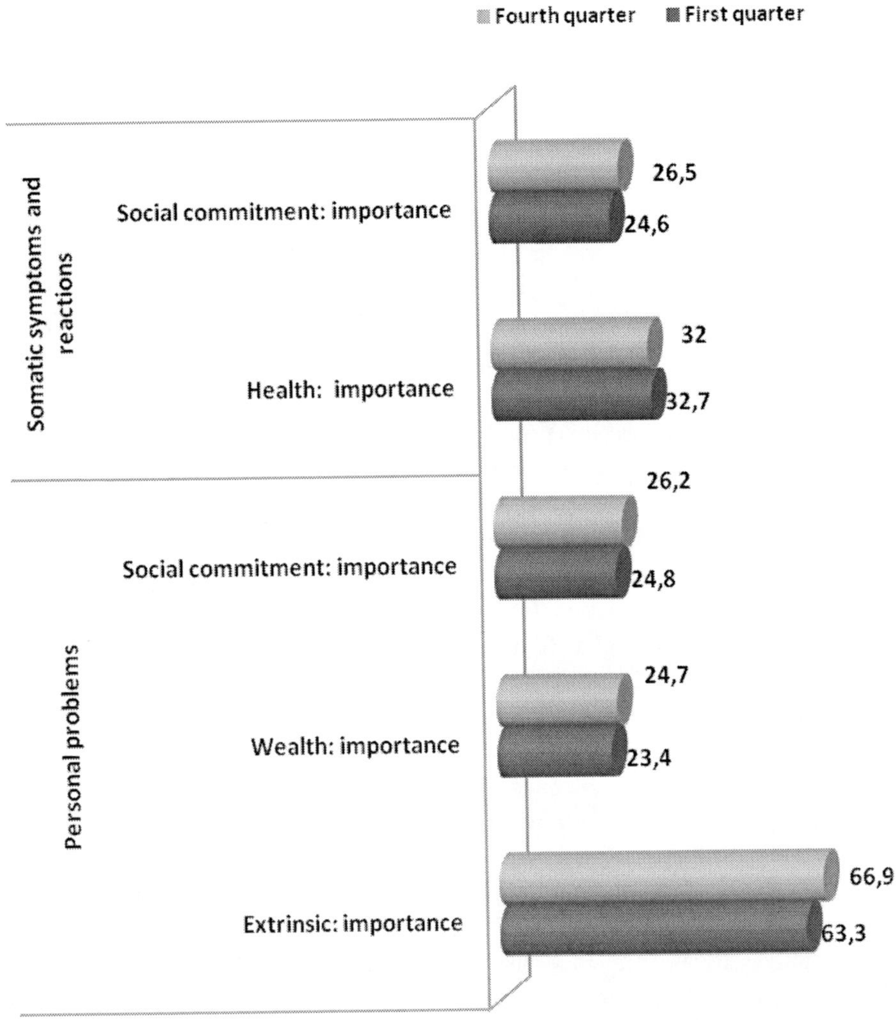

Figure 4. The averages of the significant differences in personal aspirations between the test groups created according to their results achieved on the scales of personal problems and somatic symptoms and complaints of Grob's "disease existence" scale.

Students who are more satisfied with life from the aspects of the likelihood and realization of their personal aspirations (as measured on Diener' Life Satisfaction Scale and Grob's dimension of satisfaction), considered the present realization and the potential of the future realization of all their personal aspirations (whether intrinsic or extrinsic) significantly better ($p<0.000$) than students who are less satisfied with their life.

Out of the indicators of Grob's Disease Existence, the likelihood and realization of personal problems and somatic symptoms and complaints have been found to be in a close connection with intrinsic aspirations. Participants scoring low on these scales found the present realization and the potential of the future realization of all their intrinsic aspirations (except social responsibility) significantly better ($p<0.000$) than students struggling with personal problems and somatic complaints.

3.3. Interrelation between Individual Aspirations and Subjective Well-Being

The intensity of connection between the specific aspirations and the specific indicators of subjective well-being is summed up in Chart 4.

Satisfaction with life as a goal has been found to be in the closest correlation with intrinsic aspirations. In addition to that, image, health and social responsibility have also been found in a positive connection with satisfaction with life.

Szondy [13] has also found fame to be in close correlation with satisfaction with life in adolescents. A positive attitude towards life was in close correlation with the combined indicator of intrinsic aspirations and, within that, the importance of social relations. A not-so-close, but still significant, connection, was observable with health as an objective.

Out of the extrinsic aspirations, fame and image were in a relatively close correlation with that indicator of well-being. Self-esteem was found to be in close correlation with the combined indicator of intrinsic aspirations. Within that, a not-so-close, but still significant, connection was observed with social responsibility. Pleasure in life was in close connection with the importance of both intrinsic and extrinsic aspirations. Out of intrinsic aspirations, social relations and health, while out of the extrinsic aspirations, image and fame were in close connection with this particular indicator of subjective well-being.

Depressive mood has been found to be in a positive connection with social relations and wealth, and in a close negative connection with the importance of health and the combined indicator of intrinsic aspirations. Personal problems showed the closest connection with social responsibility. In addition to that, a relatively close correlation has been observed with the importance of extrinsic aspirations and, within that, fame and image. The somatic symptoms and reactions were in the closest connection also with the importance of social responsibility, and in a not-so-close negative correlation with the importance of health.

The probability of the individuals fulfilling their personal aspirations has been found in a close relationship with the indicators of subjective well-being we examined. The connection between the likelihood of the specific aspirations and the indicators of subjective well-being is shown in Chart 5.

Satisfaction with life according to Diener has been in a positive correlation with the likelihood of achieving all the aspirations, with personal advancement and meaningful social connections on the top of the list.

Szondy [13] found the same tendency in adolescents. All the four of Grob's satisfaction indicators showed a close correlation with the likelihood of achieving all the personal aspirations. A positive attitude towards life, self-esteem, and pleasure in life were all in a positive relation with the personal aspirations. Within that, the correlation was the closest with the likelihood of personal advancement in all three, followed by the combined indicator of intrinsic aspirations and meaningful personal connections.

Depressive mood has also been found in a significant correlation with all the personal aspirations, but the nature of this connection has been negative in each case. The intensity of the connections appeared to be the same as in the case of the Grob-indicators discussed earlier, except that in this case the likelihood of health was stronger than that of meaningful human relations. Out of the indicators of Grob's disease existence, those of personal problems was in a negative significant connection of the combined intrinsic aspirations and, within that, with the likelihood of personal advancement, health, and meaningful human relations, and with wealth out of extrinsic aspirations. The same tendency has been observed with the indicators of somatic symptoms and reactions, to which the less intensive, but still significant, correlation with the likelihood of image was added.

The realization of the personal aspirations was also found to be in close connection with the indicators of subjective well-being we examined (Chart 6).

The indicators of Diener's life satisfaction scale and Grob's satisfaction scale were in a close positive connection with all the personal aspirations. The level of satisfaction was foreseeable not only at intrinsic aspirations (especially the realization of personal advancement) but also at extrinsic aspirations (particularly the realization of image and wealth).

Chart 4. Correlations between the importance of aspirations and the indicators of subjective well-being

	1	2	3	4	5	6	7
Wealth	-0.035	-0.027	0.096	-0.007	-0.016	0.130**	0.029
Reputation	0.058	0.075*	0.109**	0.036	0.031	0.032	0.111**
Image	0.125**	0.086*	0.093**	0.015	0.060	-0.020	0.127**
Personal advancement	-0.009	0.039	-0.039	0.038	0.071	-0.037	0.068
Personal relationships	0.101	0.118**	0.023	0.004	0.086*	0.144**	0.191**
Social commitment	0.109**	0.067	0.119**	0.104**	0.040	-0.090	0.137
Health	0.110**	0.096*	-0.008	-0.095*	0.164**	-0.140**	0.142**
Intrinsic	0.156**	0.147**	0.062	0.021	0.158**	-0.170**	0.222**
Extrinsic	0.064	0.067	0.107**	0.006	0.037	0.028	0.116**

1= Diener's Satisfaction with Life Scale, 2= Positive attitude towards life, 3= Personal problems, 4= Somatic symptoms and reactions, 5= Self-esteem, 6= Depressive mood, 7= Pleasure of life.

*=$p<0.05$, **$p<0.01$.

Chart 5. The connection between the likelihood of the specific aspirations and the indicators of subjective well-being

	1	2	3	4	5	6	7
Wealth	0.301**	0.352**	-0.115**	-0.128**	0.275**	-0.207**	0.295**
Reputation	0.229**	0.274**	-0.008	-0.009	0.205**	-0.131**	0.295**
Image	0.334**	0.333**	-0.045	-0.083*	0.305**	-0.209**	0.309**
Personal advancement	0.450**	0.555**	-0189**	-0.181**	0.539**	-0.462**	0.452**
Personal relationships	0.408**	0.445**	-0126**	-0.098**	0.395**	-0.381**	0.430**
Social commitment	0.266**	0.263**	0.044	0.062	0.191**	-0.249**	0.254**
Health	0.340**	0.357**	-0.175**	-0.250**	0.370**	-0.371**	0.302**
Intrinsic	0.455**	0.490**	-0128**	-0.144**	0.459**	-0.459**	0.449**
Extrinsic	0.323**	0.348**	-0.051	-0.069	0.292**	-0.196**	0.326**

1= Diener's Satisfaction with Life Scale, 2= Positive attitude towards life, 3= Personal problems, 4= Somatic symptoms and reactions, 5= Self-esteem, 6= Depressive mood, 7= Pleasure of life.

*=p<0.05, **p<0.01.

Chart 6. Correlations between the realization of the aspirations and the specific indicators of subjective well-being

	1	2	3	4	5	6	7
Wealth	0.371**	0.300**	-0.076*	-0.089*	0.205**	-0.153**	0.260**
Reputation	0.236**	0.243**	0.041	-0.012	0.193**	-0.117**	0.232**
Image	0.354**	0.335**	0.043	-0.092*	0.311**	-0.206**	0.330**
Personal advancement	0.488**	0.496**	-0.140**	-0.147**	0.496**	-0.402**	0.437**
Personal relationships	0.229**	0.218**	-0.067	-0.043	0.230**	-0.201**	0.220**
Social commitment	0.260**	0.229**	0.061	0.017	0.159**	-0.180**	0.232**
Health	0.318**	0.298**	-0.183**	-0.299**	0.322**	-0.290**	0.271**
Intrinsic	0.437**	0.413**	-0.087*	-0.156**	0.408**	-0.357**	0.414**
Extrinsic	0.379**	0.340**	-0.019	-0.068	0.277**	-0.182**	0.329**

1= Diener's Satisfaction with Life Scale, 2= Positive attitude towards life, 3= Personal problems, 4= Somatic symptoms and reactions, 5= Self-esteem, 6= Depressive mood, 7= Pleasure of life.

*=$p<0.05$, **$p<0.01$.

Out of Grob's disease existence indicators, those of the personal problems was in a powerful negative connection with the realization of health and personal advancement, and a less intensive, but still significant, connection with the combined intrinsic aspirations and the realization of wealth. The same tendency was observed in the indicator of somatic symptoms and reactions, except that in this indicator, there appeared to be a closer connection with the combined indicator of intrinsic aspirations.

In the following part of the research, a linear regression analysis (stepwise method) was carried out for the entire sample and for the two genders separately, in a breakdown according to each of the indicators of subjective well-being, using the importance, likelihood, and realization of the specific individual aspirations as predictors.

The results of the regression analysis of Diener's life satisfaction inventory are summed up in Chart 7.

Chart 7. The regression of satisfaction with life to the scales of the Aspirations Inventory (approved models; p<0.05)

Predictor	Béta	t	p<
Total: $F_{totál}$*=95,179; df=3/712; p<0.000*			
Personal advancement: realization	0.359	9,557	0.000
Personal relationships: probability	0.327	7,105	0.000
Personal relationships: importance	-0.155	-3,811	0.000
Women: $F_{totál}$*=79,475; df=3/545; p<0.000*			
Personal advancement: realization	0.404	8,263	0.000
Intrinsic: probability	0.281	5,620	0.000
Social commitment: realization	-0.122	-2,724	0.007
Men: $F_{totál}$*=21,229; df=3/167; p<0.000*			
Image: probability	0.382	3,989	0.000
Intrinsic: realization	0.323	3,867	0.000
Extrinsic: importance	-0.254	-3,063	0.007

In the entire sample, satisfaction with life has been found to be in a close positive correlation with the realized personal advancement and the likelihood of meaningful human relations, and in a considerably negative one with the importance of meaningful human relations, explaining a total of 29.6% of the variance. A person, therefore, appears to be more satisfied with his/her life when his/her personal advancement is realized, and in the future, meaningful human relations are expected, but the person regards the importance of these connections less important when assessing his/her own person.

When the two genders are examined separately, personal aspirations explain 31.5% of the variance of satisfaction with life in the case of women. A positive significant connection was found with the realization of personal advancement and the likelihood of the combined indicator of intrinsic aspirations, and a negative significant relation with the realization of social commitment. In the case of men, personal aspirations were responsible for 28.7% of the variance of satisfaction with life. Positive significant connection was found in the likelihood of image and the realization of the combined intrinsic aspirations, and a negative significant connection with the importance of combined extrinsic aspirations. It means that satisfaction with life is different for men and women. For women, the source of satisfaction is the realized personal advancement, coupled with the likelihood of intrinsic aspirations and some realized social commitment; for men, satisfaction is rooted primarily in a good future image and good appearance; resting on already-realized intrinsic aspirations, the extrinsic aspirations do not usually constitute important goals in life.

The results of the regression analysis for positive attitude to life out of Grob's satisfaction indicators are summed up in Chart 8.

Chart 8. The regression of positive attitude to life for the scales of the Aspirations Inventory (approved models; p<0.05)

Predictor	Béta	T	p<
Total: $F_{totál}$=112,826; df=3/712; p<0.000			
Personal advancement: probability	0.306	6,309	0.000
Personal advancement: realization	0.204	4,637	0.000
Personal relationships: probability	0.151	3,748	0.000
Women: $F_{totál}$=84,975; df=3/545; p<0.000			
Personal advancement: probability	0.308	5,564	0.000
Personal advancement: realization	0.206	4,084	0.000
Personal relationships: probability	0.142	3,097	0.002
Men: $F_{totál}$=37,389; df=3/167; p<0.000			
Personal advancement: probability	0.329	4,495	0.000
Personal relationships: realization	0.234	3,420	0.001
Extrinsic: probability	0.228	3,004	0.003

In the entire sample, a positive attitude toward life has been found to be in a positive correlation with the likelihood and realization of personal advancement and with the likelihood of meaningful human relations, all of these explaining 33.2% of the variance.

A positive attitude toward life is more characteristic of a person when the likelihood of his/her personal advancement is higher (for that the foundation is the already realized personal advancement) and the more chances the individual has for meaningful human relations in the future.

When examining the two genders separately, personal aspirations explained a greater part of the variance of positive attitude (41.5%) in the case of men. Positive significant correlation was observed with the likelihood of personal advancement, the realization of meaningful personal relations, and the likelihood of combined extrinsic aspirations.

In the case of women, personal aspirations explained 32.9% of the variance of positive attitude toward life. Positive significant connection was found with the likelihood of personal advancement, the realization of personal advancement, and the likelihood of meaningful human relations.

While in the case of women, the tendency of a positive attitude toward life was valid for the entire group, in the case of men, the likelihood of extrinsic aspirations and already-realized meaningful human relations were added to the likelihood of personal advancement in the emergence of a positive attitude toward life.

The results of the regression analysis for self-esteem are summed up in Chart 9.

In the entire sample, there was a positive significant correlation between self-esteem and the likelihood and realization of personal advancement, and a negative significant correlation with social commitment, all of these explaining 33.2% of the variance. A person's self-esteem will, therefore, be higher if the likelihood of his/her personal advancement is higher (for that the foundation is the already-realized personal advancement), and the level of social commitment of the individual concerned is lower.

In self-esteem, personal aspirations explained almost identical proportions of the variance in both genders (men: 36.5%, women: 34.6%). In the case of men, there was a positive significant correlation with the likelihood of personal advancement and the realization of image, and a negative significant correlation with the realization of wealth.

In the case of women, there was a positive significant correlation with the likelihood and realization of personal advancement, and a negative significant correlation with the realization of social commitment. While in the case of women, the tendencies in self-esteem were valid for the entire group, in the case of the self-esteem of men, the realization of image (good appearance) and wealth were added to the important factors.

Chart 9. The regression of self-esteem for the scales of the Aspirations Inventory (approved models; p<0.05)

Predictor	Béta	T	p<
Total: $F_{totál}$=112,945; df=3/712; p<0.000			
Personal advancement: probability	0.354	8,104	0.000
Personal advancement: realization	0.325	6,659	0.000
Social commitment: realization	-0.132	-3,564	0.000
Women: $F_{totál}$=91,870; df=3/545; p<0.000			
Personal advancement: probability	0.341	6,889	0.000
Personal advancement: realization	0.315	6,460	0.000
Social commitment: realization	-0.153	-3,700	0.000
Men: $F_{totál}$=30,253; df=3/167; p<0.000			
Personal advancement: probability	0.436	6,292	0.000
Image: realization	0.359	4,294	0.000
Wealth: realization	-0.165	-2,091	0.038

The results of the regression analysis for the pleasures of life are summed up in Chart 10.

Chart 10. The regression of the pleasures of life for the scales of the Aspirations Inventory (approved models; p<0.05)

Predictor	Béta	T	p<
Total: $F_{totál}$=82,382, df=3/712; p<0.000			
Personal advancement: realization	0.278	7,179	0.000
Personal relationships: probability	0.260	6,987	0.000
Reputation: probability	0.107	3,066	0.002
Women: $F_{totál}$=82,172; df=2/545; p<0.000			
Personal advancement: realization	0.279	5,252	0.000
Personal advancement: probability	0.253	4,765	0.000
Men: $F_{totál}$=44,413; df=2/167; p<0.000			
Personal relationships: probability	0.384	4,951	0.000
Image: realization	0.289	3,729	0.000

In the entire sample, there was a positive significant correlation between the pleasures of life and the likelihood of personal advancement and the likelihood of meaningful human relations and the likelihood of fame, all of these explaining 26.6% of the variance. A person will, therefore, find more pleasure in life if his/her personal advance is realized and he/she sees a chance for establishing meaningful human relations and acquiring fame in the future.

Personal aspirations explained a greater part of the variance in the pleasures of life in the case of men (35.8%). There was a positive significant connection with the likelihood of meaningful human relations and the realization of image. In the case of women, personal aspirations explained 24% of the variance in the pleasures of life. Positive significant relation was found with the likelihood and realization of personal advancement.

It means that men and women have different ideas about the pleasures of life. Women regard life joyful if they have already realized some of their personal advancements and can see chance of doing that in the future, as well. Men, on the other hand, believe the pleasure of life is derived from future meaningful human relations that are based upon a good appearance and image.

The results of the regression analysis for depressive mood are summed up in Chart 11.

Chart 11. The regression of regressive mood for the scales of the Aspirations Inventory (approved models; p<0.05)

Predictor	Béta	T	p<
Total: $F_{totál}$=61,620, df=4/712; p<0.000			
Intrinsic: probability	-0.418	-9,293	0.000
Personal advancement: realization	-0.242	-5,465	0.000
Social commitment: realization	0.159	3,850	0.000
Extrinsic: importance	0.123	3,633	0.000
Women: $F_{totál}$=51,442; df=3/545; p<0.000			
Personal advancement: probability	-0.318	-5,951	0.000
Personal advancement: realization	-0198	-3,695	0.000
Extrinsic: importance	0.128	3,296	0.001
Men: $F_{totál}$=36,834; df=2/167; p<0.000			
Intrinsic: probability	-0.607	-8,492	0.000
Extrinsic: importance	0.159	2,226	0.027

In the entire sample, depressive mood has been found to be in a negative significant correlation with the combined indicator of the likelihood of intrinsic aspirations and the realization of personal advancement, and in a positive significant connection with the realization of social commitment and the combined indicator of the importance of extrinsic aspirations, all together explaining 26.6% of the variance.

A person is, therefore, able to avoid depressive mood if he/she finds it possible to realize his/her intrinsic aspirations (especially his/her personal advancement), has not undertaken any social commitment so far, and does not ascribe much importance to extrinsic aspirations.

When examining the two genders separately, a greater part of the variance of depressive mood was explained by personal aspirations (31.7%) in the case of men. Negative significant correlation was found with the likelihood of combined intrinsic aspirations, and positive significant connection with the importance of the combined extrinsic aspirations.

In the case of women, personal aspirations were responsible for 22.9% of the variance of depressive mood. A negative significant connection was found with the likelihood and realization of personal advancement, and a positive significant correlation with the importance of the combined extrinsic aspirations.

Women will be able to avoid depressive mood if they have already realized a certain personal advancement and can, therefore, see a chance for continuing that in the future. Men will be able to avoid depressive mood when they can see a good chance of realizing their intrinsic aspirations in the future.

In both genders, the lack of a depressive mood is usually coupled with a low significance attributed to the realization of extrinsic aspirations.

The results of the regression analysis for the personal problems out of the indicators of Grob's disease existence are summed up in Chart 12.

Chart 12. The regression of personal problems for the scales of the Aspirations Inventory (approved models; p<0.05)

Predictor	Béta	T	p<
Total: $F_{totál}$*=18,044, df=3/712; p<0.000*			
Personal advancement: probability	-0.228	-6,014	0.000
Social commitment: importance	0.156	4,063	0.000
Extrinsic: importance	0.109	2,884	0.000
Women: $F_{totál}$*=11,810; df=3/545; p<0.000*			
Personal advancement: probability	-0.231	-5,175	0.000
Reputation: importance	0.124	2,897	0.004
Social commitment: realization	0.113	2,518	0.012
Men: $F_{totál}$*=13,507; df=2/167; p<0.000*			
Social commitment: importance	0.344	4,468	0.000
Personal advancement: probability	-0.294	-3,828	0.000

In the entire sample, personal problems have been found to be in a negative significant correlation with the likelihood of personal advancement and in a positive significant connection with the realization of social commitment, and the combined indicator of extrinsic aspirations, all together explaining 7.4% of the variance.

A person, therefore, tends to have more personal problems if he/she believes that the chances of his/her personal advancement are diminishing, and, at the same time, the individual has social commitments and wishes to realize his/her extrinsic aspirations.

In the two genders, personal aspirations explain a larger part of the variance of personal problems of women (25.3%). A negative significant correlation has been identified with the likelihood of personal advancement, and a positive significant relation with the importance of fame and the realization of social commitment.

Personal aspirations explain a 14.5% of the variance of personal problems of men (25.3%). The personal aspirations were found to be in a positive significant connection with the importance of social commitment and in a negative significant correlation with the likelihood of personal advancement. In the case of women, the reasons for personal problems may also be fame as an objective to be attained and social commitment already realized, in addition to the diminishing likelihood of personal advancement.

In the case of men, the reasons for personal problems may be social commitment as an objective to be attained and the diminishing likelihood of personal advancement.

Chart 13. The regression of somatic symptoms and reactions for the scales of the Aspirations Inventory (approved models; p<0.05)

Predictor	Béta	T	P<
Total: $F_{totál}$*=43,196; df=2/712; p<0.000*			
Health: realization	-0.340	-9,277	0.000
Social commitment: realization	0.164	4,149	0.000
Women: $F_{totál}$*=35,467; df=2/545; p<0.000*			
Health: realization	-0.372	-8,388	0.000
Social commitment: realization	0.154	3,472	0.001
Men: $F_{totál}$*=13,074; df=3/167; p<0.000*			
Health: realization	-0.339	-4,113	0.000
Wealth: realization	0.252	3,248	0.001
Health: probability	-0.188	-2,432	0.016

The results of the regression analysis for the somatic symptoms and reactions are summed up in Chart 13.

In the entire sample, the somatic symptoms and reactions were found to be in a negative significant connection with health and in a positive significant relation with realized social commitments, these explaining 11.2% of the variance. The chances of the emergence of somatic symptoms may, therefore, increase if the person does not feel healthy and at the same time has social commitments.

In the two genders, personal aspirations explained a larger part of the variance of somatic symptoms and reactions in the case of men (19.9%). A negative significant correlation was found with the importance of health, and a positive significant connection with the realization of wealth.

In women, personal aspirations only explain 11.9% of the variance of somatic symptoms and reactions. A negative significant correlation was observable with health, and a positive significant connection with the realization of social commitments. So, in both genders, somatic symptoms are more likely to emerge if the individual does not feel healthy.

Factors that make the situation even more serious may include the realization of social commitment for women and the realization of wealth and the ignorance of the importance of health for men.

4. Conclusion

In the course of our research, we examined subjective well-being and personal aspirations on a sample of college students.

In subjective well-being—in accordance with our initial hypothesis—we did not observe any considerable difference. The only exceptions to that were identified in somatic symptoms and reactions, as women were found to be more susceptible to these reactions than men. These results are in full harmony with the findings of other research programs [2, 13].

In our second hypothesis, the prevalence of individual aspirations, we had assumed that—similar to the results of the research of V. Komlósi et al. [14] conducted on a representative Hungarian sample—college students would find intrinsic objectives, and within those, health, personal relations and social relations, the most important. Our research findings suggest that college students also tend to favor intrinsic aspirations over the extrinsic aspirations. In compliance with the findings of V. Komlósi at al. [14], college students found health, personal growth, and social relations the most important personal aspirations. They found the extrinsic aspirations, reputation, wealth, and image, as the least important objectives in life.

We have also been able to confirm our third initial hypothesis, that is, there would be a considerable difference between the genders in terms of individual aspirations, as women would find image, whereas men would find wealth, as important goals in life, as suggested by the findings of V. Komlósi et al. [14] earlier. In the sample of college students, however, men—unlike earlier findings with Hungarian samples—gave priority to reputation over wealth, which is different from the list of importance set up by women.

In a research conducted in Hungary by V. Komlósi et al. [14], it was found that women put social relations directly after health on the list of intrinsic aspirations, whereas, for men, the most important ambition was personal growth. Our fourth hypothesis was that it was going to be the same with college students. We found the domination of intrinsic aspirations in both genders, with only slight shifts of emphasis. For women, health, social relations, and personal growth was the order; for men personal advancement was on the top of the list, followed by health and social relations. These results are in full compliance with the results of V. Komlósi et al. [14].

Based upon our earlier research [9], we assumed in our fifth hypothesis that intrinsic will increase, whereas the extrinsic ones will diminish the level of subjective well-being. In accordance with our expectations, we found a close positive correlation between intrinsic aspirations and satisfaction with life, a positive attitude towards life, self-esteem, and the pleasure of life as indicators of subjective well-being, and a close negative correlation with depressive mood, personal problems, and symptoms and complaints.

Within the intrinsic aspirations, there appeared to be a slight shift of emphasis among certain personal endeavors and indicators subjective well-being. While in the case of satisfaction with life and self-esteem, health and social responsibility were important, in a positive attitude towards life and the pleasure of life, meaningful human relations and health were found to be of importance.

In the course of our research, we were, however, unable to convincingly prove the negative effect of extrinsic aspirations on subjective well-being. Although we found a close positive correlation with depressive mood and the efforts aimed at becoming rich, and between personal problems and the importance of fame and image, fame and image appeared to be in close positive relationship with the pleasure of life and satisfaction as well. Szondy [13] also identified a close correlation between satisfaction with life and the importance of fame at late adolescent age.

Our research justified our sixth hypothesis; that is, the likelihood and realization of both intrinsic and extrinsic aspirations are in close correlation with satisfaction with life as a component of subjective well-being [13]. It was verified in Diener's life satisfaction scale and Grob's satisfaction indicators, as well.

Our research findings also confirmed our seventh hypothesis; that is, all of the three levels of individual aspirations (importance, likelihood, and realization) are in close correlation with certain indicators of subjective well-being.

In general, we may conclude that there was a closer correlation between individual aspirations and certain indicators of subjective well-being in the case of men.

Individual aspirations—regardless of gender—were found to be in the closest correlation with a positive attitude towards life and self-esteem, explaining more than 33.2 % of the variance.

Both of these indicators of subjective well-being were in the closest correlation with intrinsic aspirations, particularly with the likelihood and realization of personal advancement. In self-esteem, realized social commitment, and in a positive attitude towards life, the likelihood of establishing personal relations in the future were also present.

Individual aspirations were found to be in the most remote correlation with Grob's disease existence indicators, amounting to 11.2% of the variance of somatic symptoms and complaints, and a mere 7.4% of the variance of personal problems. Somatic symptoms and complaints were in close interrelationship with the lack of health and realized social commitment, whereas personal problems were in similar relationship with diminished chances of personal advancement, social commitment as an objective, and the realization of extrinsic aspirations.

References

[1] Urbán, R. (1995). Boldogság, személyiség és egészség. [Happiness, personality and health.] *Magyar Pszichológiai Szemle. 35*, 379-404.

[2] Diener, E., & Such, E.M., & Lucas, R.E., & Smith, H.L. (1999). Subjective well-being: three decades of progress. *Psychology Bulletin. 125,* 276-302.

[3] Diener, E. (2000). Subjective well-being: the science of happiness and a proposal for a national index. *American Psychologist. 55*, 34-43.

[4] Lu, L., & Shih, J.B. (1997). Personality and happiness: is mental health a mediator? *Personality and Individual Differences. 22*, 249-256.

[5] Brebner, J., & Donaldson, J., & Kirby, N., & Ward, L. (1995). Relationship between happiness and personality. *Personality and Individual Differences. 19*, 251-258.

[6] Chan, R., & Joseph, S. (2000). Dimensions of personality, domains of aspirations, and subjective well-being. *Personality and Individual Differences. 28*, 347-354.

[7] Emmons, R. A. (1986). Personal strivings: an approach to personality and subjective well-being. *Journal of Personality and Social Psychology. 51*, 1058-1068.

[8] Brunstein, J.C. (1993). Personal goals and subjective well-being: a longitudinal study. *Journal of Personality and Social Psychology. 65*, 1061-1070.

[9] Kasser, T., & Ryan, R.M. (1993). A dark side of the American dream: correlates of financial success as a central life aspiration. *Journal of Personality and Social Psychology. 65,* 410-422.

[10] Kasser, T., & Ryan, R.M. (1996), Further examining the American dream: differential correlates of intrinsic and extrinsic goals. *Personality and Social Psychology Bulletin. 22,* 280-287.

[11] Emmons, R.A., & Diener, E. (1985): Personality correlates of subjective well-being. *Personality and Social Psychology Bulletin. 11*, 89-97.

[12] Diener, E., & Fujita (1995). Recources, personal strivings, and subjective well-being: a nomothetic and idiographic approach. *Journal of Personality and Social Psychology. 68,* 926-935.

[13] Szondy, M. (2004). A szubjektív jóllét és a törekvések kapcsolata késői serdülőkorban. [Interrelation between subjective well-being and aspirations at late adolescent.] *Alkalmazott Pszichológia. 4,* 53-72.

[14] V. Komlósi, A., & Rózsa S., & Bérdi M., & Móricz É., & Horváth D. (2006). Az Aspirációs Index hazai alkalmazásával szerzett tapasztalatok. [Experiences obtained with the domestic application of the Aspiration Index.] *Magyar Pszichológiai Szemle. 61,* 237-250.

[15] Martos, T., & Szabó G., & Rózsa S. (2006). Az Aspirációs Index rövidített változatának pszichometriai jellemzői hazai mintán. [Psychometric characteristics of the abridged Aspiration Index with domestic sample.] *Mentálhigiéné és Pszichoszomatika. 7,* 171-191.

[16] Grob, A. (1995). Subjective well-being and significant life-events across the lifespan. *Swiss Journal of Psychology. 54*, 3-18.

[17] Sallay, H. (2004): Entering the job market: belief in a just world, fairness and well-being of graduation students. In C. Dalbert, & H. Sallay (Eds.), *The Justice Motive in Adolescence and Young Adulthood: Origins and Consequences.* (pp. 215-231). Routledge, London: Routledge.

[18] Deci, E. L., & Ryan, R. M. (1985). *Intrinsic Motivation and Self-determination in Human Behavior.* New York: Plenum.
[19] Deci, E. L., & Ryan, R. M. (2000). The "what" and "why" of goal pursuits: human needs and the self-determination of behaviour. *Psychological Inquiry. 11*, 227-268.

Chapter 2

CORRELATION BETWEEN INDIVIDUAL ASPIRATIONS AND DEPRESSION

ABSTRACT

The aim of our survey was to reveal the individual aspirations among college students, which may play an important role as protective factors in the preservation of mental health, particularly regarding sub-clinical depressive syndromes. There were 712 college students involved in the study. (545 females and 167 males). The abridged version of Beck's Depression Inventory was used for the definition of the rate of depression, while the Aspiration Inventory was used to measure the rate of individual aspirations. In the course of estimating the importance of individual aspirations, we found intrinsic aspirations to be predominating in the case of college students for both genders, with a minor shifting of weight. While in the case of women, health, social relationships, and personal advancement were listed in this order of importance, in the case of men, personal advancement was listed in the first position, followed by the categories of health and social relationships. From among the symptoms of depression, social reservation was in the closest correlation with the importance of certain personal strivings, and within these, with the lack of intrinsic aspirations was highlighted. Certain symptoms of depression—regardless of generic affiliations—showed a very close correlation with the probability of nearly every personal aspiration as well as with the realisation thereof, and within this, they were in a stronger correlation with the intrinsic aspirations than with those of extrinsic ones (in the case of men, a stronger correlation between the probability of every aspiration for depressive syndromes and the realisation thereof were also found to be stronger than in the case of women). Examining the overall correlation between all the three categories of individual aspirations (importance, probability, realisation), in the case of depression, we found that depression showed a close negative correlation with the probability of personal growth and social relationships and the realisation of health, while a positive correlation was detected with the importance attributed to intrinsic aspirations, which explained almost one-fourth of the variances of depression altogether. The depressive syndromes found to be typical of college students (worthlessness, fatigue, hesitation, hopelessness, dissatisfaction) showed a much closer correlation with the importance, probability, and realisation of individual aspirations in the case of men than in the case of women. From among the aforementioned symptoms of depression, individual aspirations had the closest correlation with hopelessness in the case of both genders. While in the case of men, the importance of intrinsic aspirations and the current dissatisfaction of these may lead principally to the development of hopelessness, for women, the development of the feeling of hopelessness is primarily correlated with an extrinsic aspiration, the importance of wealth, and the current lack thereof. In the case of the rest of the depressive syndromes, the explanatory power of the correlation with individual aspirations was different for women and men.

1. Introduction

1.1. Individual Aspirations and Depression

In our days, health psychology is based upon a dynamic approach to the personality. In this way, psychology does not primarily deal with the interrelation between the constant features of the personality and health, but interprets the human personality as a functional system, in which perceptions, cognitions, values, and personal ambitions constitute an organic whole, exerting their joint effect on health. In view of all of this, it is necessary to identify the personal goals, values, and aspirations that may serve as a protective factor in preserving health, creating and maintaining psychic balance, and contributing to the elimination or counterbalancing of undesired behavior patterns. In this volume, the authors make an effort to find the answers to these questions. The authors examine the connections of personal aspirations with subjective well-being and certain depression symptoms [1].

What has been described above may raise the question as to what objectives, values, and aspirations play the most important protective role in preserving our health and maintaining our psychic balance and helping us to avoid, or compensate for, unacceptable behavior patterns? [2].

Researchers do not seem to be keen on asking this question in connection with the so-called positive or negative values. Deciding the question obviously requires a value judgment that researchers are reluctant to make. Most of the theories and models do not contain pre-suppositions as to what values are "healthier" than others, and do not attempt to combine the various values with psychological variables such as subjective well-being, optimum performance, the development of the self, or the negative or positive forms of health behavior [2].

Out of the process models of health behavior, it is Deci and Ryan's [3] self-determination theory—making a distinction between intrinsic and extrinsic values and aspirations—that offers a theoretical background for answering the question. In this theory, aspirations for intrinsic values offer an internal satisfaction, as they are directly connected to basic human values such as a need for autonomy, competence, and social relations. Intrinsic values are based upon people's real spiritual needs; they support the mental development of the individual. These internal values include personal endeavors and motivations aimed at self-acceptance, personal advancement, interpersonal connections/intimacy and social feelings.

As opposed to these, extrinsic values satisfy psychological needs in a less direct way, and they often co-occur with a lower or inflated, fragile and uncertain, so-called contingent (conditional) self-esteem, psychological uncertainty, and openness to activities that are directly harmful or do not offer any pleasure. They also co-occur with an openness to external pressure and influence. As the extrinsic values are not based upon the individual's basic psychological needs, the individual tends to seek such values outside his/her own personality, and gaining these values is often subject to the confirmation and approval by other people. Extrinsic values include the powerfully propagated objectives and values of the consumer society, such as money and material wealth, our proper image in the eyes of others, the importance of good appearance, and being well-known and accepted in society [4].

When an individual concentrates on such external values, he/she places the source of satisfaction outside him/herself, so these values do not simply fail to support the mental development of the individual, but they may cause a bad mood, a higher level of tension, and the difficulties associated with coping with this situation [4].

Kasser and Ryan [5], when examining the connections between objectives, values, and subjective well-being, found that the persons for whom the extrinsic goals were important (financial successes, money, and material wealth) reported a lower level of well-being and were in a worse mental state, regardless of their gender, than those to whom intrinsic objectives (accepting ourselves, relations, and community feelings) were important.

From the aspect of the individual, research has confirmed that a relative intrinsic orientation is closely connected to a number of positive individual variables, e.g., a higher level of satisfaction with life, experiencing more positive emotions, a higher level of vitality and a better general mood, and a lower level of depression and anxiety. In connection with a relative extrinsic orientation, on the other hand, the opposite of all that has been demonstrated: materialistic persons are characterized by a lower level of vitality and a higher level of depression and anxiety. Purely materialistic values come together with a generally bad mood, anti-social behavior, and narcissism [4].

According to the theory of self-determination, intrinsic values are more useful than extrinsic values for both the individual and the entire society, as sound individual values make up a soundly functioning society [3, 4].

1.2. The Aim of the Research

The purpose of our research was to survey among college students the individual aspirations that may serve as a protective factor in preserving health, with special attention to certain symptoms of sub-clinical depression.

2. Method

2.1. Participants

Data was collected among students at the College of Nyíregyháza. We collected data randomly at every faculty, and participation was voluntary and done with their consent. There were 750 students who took part in the research, and 712 of them provided valuable data (545 women and 167 men).

The average age was 19.98 (standard deviation 1.58) the median value was 20 years.

2.2. Measures

2.2.1. Survey of the Actual Symptoms of Depression

Hungarian Version of the Abridged Screening Version of Beck's Depression Inventory [6,7]

The inventory studies the following components of depressive syndromes: sadness, pessimism, sense of failure, dissatisfaction, guilt, fear of punishment, suicide thoughts, indecisiveness, social withdrawal, self-image change, work difficulty, fatigability, and anorexia.

According to the researches hitherto [8, 9], the abridged version comprising 13 items may be divided into two factors, somatic and non-somatic factors. The factors of the somatic syndromes are composed of the work difficulty, the fatigability, and anorexia.

The surveys carried out by Margitics [10] have isolated two factors within the non-somatic factor: pure depression and the feeling of guilt. The following depressive syndromes belonged to the pure depression: sadness, pessimism, sense of failure, dissatisfaction, suicide thoughts, and indecisiveness, while the feeling of guilt, fear of punishment, and social withdrawal belonged to guilt.

2.2.2. Survey of the Individual Aspirations

Hungarian Version of the Aspiration Inventory [11]

(See detailed explanation in the previous chapter.)

2.2.3. Survey of Lifetime Events

Hungarian Version of the Secondary School Lifetime Event Questionnaire

Secondary School Lifetime Event Questionnaire developed by Cohen et al., the Hungarian version adapted by Csorba et al. [12] was employed.

The questionnaire focused on the frequent, mainly negative, but sometimes partly positive, life events of the preceding six months. The questionnaire measured the following dimensions: number of positive life events, score of positive life events, number of negative life events, and score of negative life events.

The questionnaire was used for the screening of the elevated rate of depression caused by negative life events.

3. Results

3.1. Descriptive and Comparative Statistics

The descriptive statistics of the results measured according to Beck's Depression Inventory for the whole pattern and in a breakdown according to the genders are provided below (M=mean value, SD=standard deviation).

Total:

- M=6.1; SD=5.4

Women:

- M=6.3; SD=5.2

Men:

- M=5.4; SD=5.9

A comparative statistical analysis of depression in the two genders (two-paired t-test) indicates that the depression level in females is significantly higher than that of men ($t=3.124$, $p<0.000$).

The occurrence of various depression symptoms (including varieties of mild and medium-seriousness as well) within the sample is shown in Figure 1.

The figure suggests that the symptom of depression most characteristic of college students is a sense of guilt (54.4%). There were 49.9% of them who complained of fatigue, 49.4% of an inability to make decisions, 48.7% of pessimism and 47.7% of dissatisfaction. The least common of the symptoms was suicide thoughts (15%).

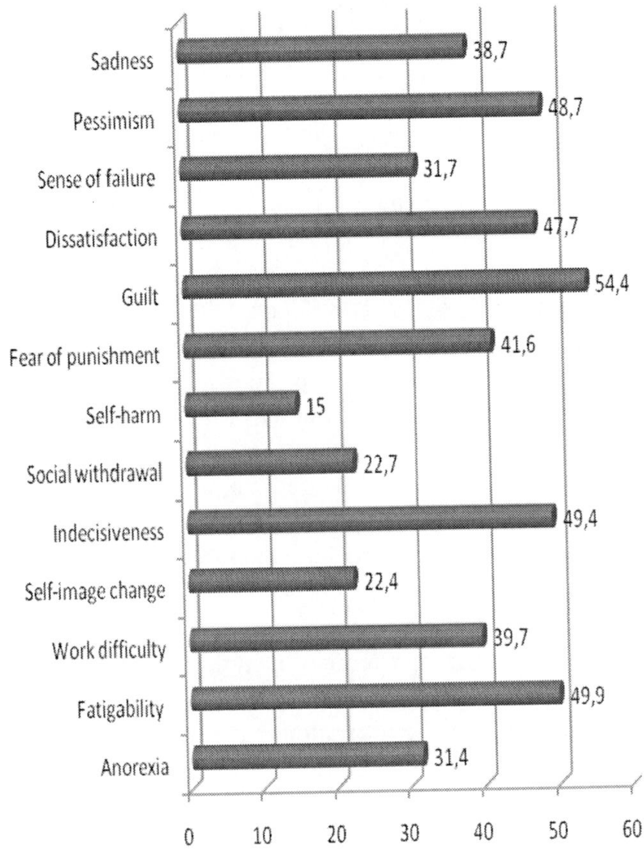

Figure 1. The occurrence rate of depressive syndromes in the complete sample as per Beck's Depression Inventory.

In a research conducted in 2004, Margitics [17] also found similar proportions in college students. The data in the chart indicate that out of the various depression symptoms (varieties of mild and medium-seriousness), college students were primarily characterized by a sense of guilt (59.6%) in 2004. Work difficulty (56%) and dissatisfaction (55.1%) also occurred in more than half of them. It was followed by a sense of inability to work (48%), pessimism (46.4%) and indecisiveness (42.9%). Out of all the symptoms, suicide thoughts (15.6%) and social withdrawal (19%) were of the lowest proportion.

3.2. Connection between Symptoms of Depression and Individual Aspirations

Within the entire sample and within the group of women, no considerable difference between the importance of the specific aspirations and depression (BDI total scores) was observable. In the case of men, there was a not very close, negative connection with social relations ($r=-0.158$, $p<0.05$).

In the entire sample, out of the symptoms of depression, social withdrawal was found to be in the closest correlation with the importance of specific personal aspirations. It was in a negative significant connection with the combined indicator of intrinsic aspirations ($r=-0.161$, $p<0.01$), social connections ($r=-0.155$, $p<0.01$), health ($r=-0.124$, $p<0.01$) and image ($r=-0.101$, $p<0.01$).

As for the other symptoms of depression, an inability to make decisions ($r=0.099$, $p<0.01$) and a sense of valuelessness ($r=0.088$, $p<0.01$) were in a close positive correlation with social commitment and hopelessness with wealth ($r=0.076$, $p<0.05$).

When examining the genders separately, we found a close correlation with more depression symptoms in the case of men than in the case of women.

In the case of men, social withdrawal was in the closest correlation with the importance of most of the aspirations. There was a negative connection with social relationships ($r=-0.235$, $p<0.01$), the combined indicator of intrinsic aspirations ($r=-0.201$, $p<0.01$), health ($r=-0.190$, $p<0.01$) and image ($r=-0.166$, $p<0.05$). Body image was also in close negative connection with social relations ($r=-0.241$, $p<0.01$), the combined indicator of intrinsic aspirations ($r=-0.218$, $p<0.01$), and health ($r=-0.167$, $p<0.05$). Less intensive, but still a significant negative correlation, was identified between failures and the importance of image ($r=0176p<0.05$).

Chart 1 contains the intensity of connection between the likelihood of certain aspirations and depression and its symptoms.

Chart 1. Correlations between the likelihood of certain aspirations and depression and its symptoms

	1	2	3	4	5	6	7	8	9
BDI Total	-0.264**	-0150**	-0.270**	-0.419**	-0.313**	-0.177**	-0.366**	-0.380**	-0.234**
Sadness	-0.188**	-0.83*	-0.136**	-0.254**	-0.213**	-0.101**	-0.207**	-0.246**	-0.159**
Pessimism	-0.249**	-0.163**	-0.203**	-0.390**	-0.276**	-0.153**	-0288**	-0.329**	-0.231**
Sense of failure	-0.227**	-0.107**	-0.170**	-0.331**	-0.271**	-0.060	-0.314**	-0.311**	-0.183**
Dissatisfaction	-0.146**	-0.130**	-0.109**	-0.293**	-0.216**	-0.057	-0.215**	-0.246**	-0.134**
Guilt	-0.144**	-0.096*	-0.133**	-0.253**	-0.177**	-0.008	-0.234**	-0.196**	-0.134**
Fear of punishment	-0.166**	-0.132**	-0.138**	-0.283**	-0.139**	-0.013	-0.182**	-0.197**	-0.177**
Suicide thoughts	-0.182**	0.091*	-0.146**	-0.268**	-0.216**	-0.098**	-0.298**	-0.289**	-0.167**
Social withdrawal	-1.18**	-0.073	-0.144**	-0.251**	-0.271**	-0.149**	-0.246**	-0.291**	-0.133**
Indecisiveness	-0.154**	-0.130**	-0.094*	-0.250**	-0.131**	0.015	-0.186**	-0176**	-0.148**
Self-image change	-0147**	-0.057	-0.150**	-0247**	-0.207**	-0.090*	-0.209**	-0.249**	-0140**
Work difficulty	-0.243**	-0.120**	-0.149**	-0.331**	-0220**	-0.158**	-0.316**	-0329**	-0187**
Fatigability	-0.148**	-0.066	-0.073	-0199**	-0181**	-0.099**	-0.230**	-0.219**	-0.095*
Anorexia	-0.044	0.009	-0.043	-0.092*	-0.042	0.034	-0.094*	-0.072	-0.031

1= Wealth, 2= Reputation, 3= Image, 4= Personal advancement, 5= Personal relationships 6= Social commitment, 7= Health, 8= Intrinsic total, 9= Extrinsic total, *=p<0.05, **p<0.01.

In the entire sample, there was a close and negative correlation between depression and the likelihood of all the aspirations concerned. The closest negative correlation was found to be between depression and likelihood of intrinsic aspirations and, within that, the likelihood of personal advancement and health. The correlation was the least intensive with social commitment. Out of the extrinsic aspirations, depression showed a more powerful connection with the likelihood of wealth and image than with fame. In the two genders, the negative correlation was more powerful with each of the aspirations in the case of men than in the case of women. In intrinsic and extrinsic aspirations, the tendency was the same for both genders (women: intrinsic $r=-0.362$, $p<0.000$, extrinsic: $r=-0.209$, $p<0.000$; men: intrinsic: $r=-0.492$, $p<0.000$; extrinsic: $r=-0.306$, $p<0.000$).

The specific depression symptoms—regardless of gender—were found to be in intensive correlation with the likelihood of almost all of the individual aspirations, more powerful with the intrinsic than with the extrinsic ones. In men, there was a more powerful connection between depression symptoms and each of the aspirations than in the case of women. The indicator of the likelihood of combined intrinsic aspirations was in a significant negative correlation with all the symptoms of depression, except the lack of appetite. The closest correlation was found between depression symptoms and personal advancement and health in the entire sample and in the case of women, whereas, in the case of men, there was a negative correlation between the lack of appetite and personal advancement. In the case of health, there was a negative correlation with all of them (with the exception of dissatisfaction and self-punishment). The likelihood of social relations, regardless of gender, was in a close, negative correlation with all the symptoms of depression, with the exception of the lack of appetite. Out of the intrinsic aspirations, the likelihood of social commitment was found to be in the least intensive connection with certain symptoms of depression.

In the entire sample, there was a close correlation with inability to work, social withdrawal, and hopelessness. In the case of women, a close relationship was observed with the inability to work ($r=-0.138$, $p<0.0019$), whereas in men, a negative correlation was identified with social withdrawal ($r=-0.276$, $p<0.000$), hopelessness ($r=-0.258$, $p<0.001$), and troubles with the image of their external appearance ($r=-0.238$, $p<0.002$). As for extrinsic aspirations, the likelihood of wealth and image was in the closest correlation with some of the symptoms of depression. Regardless of gender, there was a significant negative correlation between wealth and image and all the symptoms of depression (with the exception of the lack of appetite and fatigue). Out of the extrinsic aspirations, the likelihood of fame did not appear to be in a close correlation with certain symptoms of depression. In the case of women, the closest negative relationship was observed with self-punishment ($r=-0.155$, $p<0.000$), inability to work ($r=-0.126$, $p<0.003$), and hopelessness ($r=-0,124$, $p<0.004$); while in the case of men, the same was found with hopelessness ($r=-0.251$, $p<0.000$), failure ($r=-0.219$, $p<0.001$), and sadness ($r=-0.215$, $p<0.002$).

Chart 2 shows the intensity of the connection between the realization of certain aspirations and the symptoms of depression.

In the entire sample, there was a close negative correlation between depression and the realization of certain aspirations. When the two genders were examined separately, in the case of women, the realization of social commitment was the only element that was not in a close relationship with depression. In the case of men, the same was observed with the realization of wealth. Depression, in this case, was also found to be in a closer relationship with the intrinsic, than it was with the extrinsic aspirations. Out of realized intrinsic aspirations, the closest negative correlation was observed with personal advancement and health, and the least intensive negative relationship existed with the realization of social commitment. Out of extrinsic aspirations, the closest negative relationship existed between depression and the realization of image, and the weakest connection was observed with fame. In a breakdown according to the two genders, the negative correlation with each of the aspirations was stronger in the case of men than in women. In both the intrinsic and extrinsic aspirations, the tendency valid for the entire sample was observed in both genders. In both sexes, the realization of intrinsic aspirations was in a closer correlation with depression than the realization of extrinsic aspirations (women: intrinsic $r=-0.307$, $p<0.000$, extrinsic: $r=-0.201$, $p<0.000$; men: intrinsic: $r=-0.455$, $p<0.000$; extrinsic: $r=-0.217$, $p<0.000$).

The individual depression symptoms—regardless of gender—were in a close correlation with the realization of almost all of the individual aspirations, even closer with the intrinsic than with the extrinsic ones. In men, the correlation with the depression symptoms was more powerful than in the case women. Research into the interrelations between the realization of aspirations and the symptoms of depression provided similar results to those found in the examination of the probability of the aspirations.

Chart 2. The connection between the realization of certain aspirations and the symptoms of depression

	1	2	3	4	5	6	7	8	9
BDI Total	-0.171**	-0.132**	-0.211**	-0.381**	-0148**	-0.110**	-0.337**	-0.335**	-0.206**
Sadness	-0.142**	-0.099**	-0.160**	-0.261**	-0.106**	-0.099**	-0.204**	-0.245**	-0.160**
Pessimism	-0.163**	-0.125**	-0.203**	-0.361**	-0.128**	-0.121**	-0.281**	-0.298	-0195**
Sense of failure	-0174**	-0.132**	-0.172**	-0.338**	-0.182**	-0.086*	-0.265**	-0.289**	-0.185**
Dissatisfaction	-0.070	-0.065	-0.092*	-0242**	-0.077*	-0.042	-0.181**	-0.181**	-0.091*
Guilt	-0.078*	-0.101**	-0.134**	-0.259**	-0.092*	-0.050	-0.240**	-0.207**	-0.125**
Fear of punishment	-0116**	-0.107**	-0.151**	-0268**	-0.057	-0.027	-0.175**	-0.188**	-0.154**
Suicide thoughts	-0.136**	-0.076*	-0128**	-0.232**	-0.044	-0.071	-0.221**	-0.221**	-0.146**
Social withdrawal	-0.082*	-0.096*	-0.130**	-0203**	-0.129**	-0.077*	-0.183**	-0.203**	-0.120**
Indecisiveness	-0.079*	-0.085*	-0.098**	-0221**	-0-60	-0.023	-0.180**	-0.151**	-0.140**
Self-image change	-0.126**	-0.044	-0.162**	-0.212**	-0.107**	-0.072	-0.200**	-0.202**	-0.146**
Work difficulty	-0.120**	-0.100**	-0.129**	-0.258**	-0.050	-0.114**	-0.279**	-0.273**	-0.142**
Fatigability	-0.079*	-0.059	-0.083*	-0.188**	-0.107**	-0.103**	-0.239**	-0.202**	-0.091*
Anorexia	-0.025	0.010	-0.049	-0.057	-0.040	0.006	-0.094*	-0.083*	-0.018

1= Wealth, 2= Reputation, 3= Image, 4= Personal advancement, 5= Personal relationships 6= Social commitment, 7= Health, 8= Intrinsic total, 9= Extrinsic total, *=$p<0.05$, **$p<0.01$.

In the following part of the research, a linear regression analysis (stepwise method) of depression (BDI total score) was carried out for the entire sample and for the two genders separately. In the analysis, depression was the dependant variable, and the importance, likelihood, and realization of the aspirations as predictors. The results of the regression analysis of depression are listed in Chart 3.

Chart 3. The regression of depression (BDI total score) for the Aspiration Inventory (approved models; p<0.05)

Predictor	Béta	T	p<
Total: $F_{totál}$=53,790; df=4/712; p<0.000			
Personal advancement: probability g	-0.363	-8,037	0.000
Intrinsic: importance	0.200	5,208	0.000
Health: realization	-0.167	-4,373	0.000
Personal relationships: probability	-0.118	-2,619	0.009
Women: $F_{totál}$=41,789; df=4/545; p<0.000			
Personal advancement: realization	-0.258	-4,300	0.000
Personal advancement: probability	-0.231	-3,703	0.000
Health: realization	-0.168	-3,448	0.001
Intrinsic: importance	0.125	2,779	0.006
Men: $F_{totál}$=17,846; df=4/167; p<0.000			
Personal relationships: probability	-0.370	-4,032	0.000
Personal advancement: probability	-0.280	-3,225	0.002
Intrinsic: importance	0.247	3,220	0.002
Health: realization	-0.234	-2,987	0.003

In the entire sample, there was a close negative correlation between depression and the likelihood of personal advancement and social relations, the realization of health, and a positive correlation with the importance attributed to intrinsic aspirations, all of these explaining 24% of the variance of depression. Therefore, if a person does not feel healthy at the moment and sees no chance of personal advancement or good social relationships in the future, but regards intrinsic aspirations important, the individual will be susceptible to depressive reactions.

When the two genders are examined separately, individual aspirations were found to be in a closer correlation with depression, explaining 36% of the variance. There was negative correlation with the likelihood of social relationships and personal advancement and the realization of health, and there was a positive one with the importance of intrinsic aspirations. In men, the factors increasing the susceptibility to depressive reactions were found to be the same as in the case of the entire sample. In the case of women, individual aspirations explained a mere 24.4% of the variance of depression. The emergence of depressive reaction in the case of women was only different from the entire sample, and the tendencies observed in men in that case, the realization of personal advancement as a risk factor replaced the likelihood of future social relationships.

We carried out the linear regression analysis (stepwise method) for the depression symptoms that were characteristic of college students (see Figure 1). Depression symptoms served as dependant variables, and the importance, likelihood, and realization of individual aspirations.

Chart 4 contains the results of the regression analysis carried out for the sense of valuelessness.

Chart 4. The regression of the sense of valuelessness for the scales of the Aspiration Inventory (approved models; p<0.05)

Predictor	Béta	T	p<
Total: $F_{totál}$=18,742; df=3/712; p<0.000			
Social commitment: importance	0.165	4,169	0.000
Personal advancement: realization	-0.170	-3,365	0.001
Personal advancement: probability	-0.163	-3,192	0.001
Women: $F_{totál}$=23,183; df=2/545; p<0,000			
Personal advancement: realization	-0.223	-4,665	0.000
Social commitment: importance	0.169	4,075	0.000
Men: $F_{totál}$=8,528; df=3/167; p<0,000			
Personal advancement: realization	-0.246	-3,014	0.003
Personal advancement: probability	-0.215	-2,630	0.004
Extrinsic: importance	0.191	2,454	0.015

The individual aspirations only explained 10% of the variance of the sense of valuelessness. The sense of valuelessness was found to be in a close positive relationship with the importance of social commitment, and in a negative correlation with the likelihood and realization of personal advancement. When an individual finds social commitments important and is at the same time dissatisfied with his/her personal advancement at that given time, and when he/she sees no chance for that in the future, he/she may consider him/herself as valueless. Personal aspirations in connection with valuelessness explained the variance almost to the same extent in the two genders (men: 13.9%, women: 11.8%). In the case of men, the feeling of valuelessness may emerge from dissatisfaction with their current personal relationship, their chances of future personal advancement, and they attribute much significance to extrinsic aspirations. In the case of women, a feeling of valuelessness may crop up from dissatisfaction with their current personal advancement and they pay much attention to social commitments.

The results of the regression analysis carried out for fatigue (Chart 5) show that fatigue is in close negative correlation with the realization of health and the likelihood of intrinsic aspirations and a positive correlation with the importance of image in the whole sample, explaining 7.6% of the variance in fatigue. In the case of an individual, therefore, fatigue may arise if he/she does not feel healthy and cannot see the chance of satisfying his/her intrinsic aspirations in the future, while he/she attributes great significance to external appearance (image).

Chart 5. The regression of fatigue for the scales of the Aspiration Inventory (approved models; p<0.05)

Predictor	Béta	T	p<
Total: $F_{totál}$*=25,190; df=3/712; p<0.000*			
Health: realization	-0.178	-3,907	0.000
Intrinsic: probability	-0.139	-3,040	0.002
Image: importance	0.103	2,716	0.007
Women: $F_{totál}$*=26,024; df=1/545; p<0,000*			
Intrinsic: probability	-0.218	-5,101	0.000
Men: $F_{totál}$*=21,507; df=2/167; p<0,000*			
Health: realization	-0.475	-6,487	0.000
Extrinsic: importance	0.201	2,740	0.007

There have been major differences between the two genders in terms of the interrelations between fatigue and individual aspirations. In the case of women, personal aspirations explained a mere 4.7% of the variance of fatigue, and the respective figure was 21.3% in men. In this aspect, men may experience fatigue if they do not feel healthy and wish to satisfy their extrinsic aspirations. In the case of women, the reason was the lack of hope for satisfying their intrinsic aspirations in the future.

Chart 6 contains the results of the regression analysis carried out for the inability to make decisions.

In the entire sample, there was a close negative correlation with the realization of social commitment and a positive correlation with the importance of the intrinsic aspirations, together making up 10.3% of the variance of the inability to make decisions. According to that, a person may feel unable to make decisions when he/she believes that the level of his/her social commitments is below the expected, while he/she ascribes great importance to intrinsic aspirations. In a breakdown according to the genders, individual aspirations explained a higher proportion of the variance in the case of men (17.6%); the respective figure in the case of women was only 9.1%. In both genders, the inability to make decisions may increase if they attribute importance to intrinsic aspirations while they cannot see a chance for a personal advancement in the future. In men, indecisiveness may also increase if they believe that they have little chance for establishing partnership in the near future.

Chart 6. The regression of the inability to make decisions for the scales of the Aspiration Inventory (approved models; p<0.05)

Predictor	Béta	T	p<
Total: $F_{totál}$=39,048; df=2/712; p<0.000			
Social commitment: realization	-0.346	-8,643	0.000
Intrinsic: importance	0.214	5,352	0.000
Women: $F_{totál}$=25,952; df=2/545; p<0.000			
Personal advancement: probability	-0.326	-7,124	0.000
Intrinzik: fontosság	0.179	3,899	0.000
Men: $F_{totál}$=11,240; df=3/167; p<0,000			
Personal advancement: probability	-0.314	-3,285	0.001
Intrinsic: importance	0.285	3,386	0.001
Personal relationships: probability	-0.222	-2,286	0.024

Chart 7. The regression of hopelessness for the scales of the Aspiration Inventory (approved models; p<0.05)

Predictor	Béta	t	p<
Total: $F_{totál}$=32,180; df=3/712; p<0,000			
Personal advancement: probability	-0.332	-7,343	0.000
Intrinsic: realization	-0.266	-4,360	0.000
Intrinsic: importance	0.145	3,594	0.000
Women: $F_{totál}$=28,942; df=4/545; p<0,000			
Wealth: importance	0.243	4,567	0.000
Wealth: realization	-0.2302	-3,908	0.000
Personal advancement: realization	-0.21	-3,678	0.000
Personal advancement: probability	-0.172	-2,800	0.005
Men: $F_{totál}$=12,981; df=4/167; p<0,000			
Intrinsic: probability	-1.128	-7,094	0.000
Intrinsic: importance	0.586	4,467	0.000
Health: probability	0.538	4,347	0.000
Health: realization	-0.475	-6,487	0.000

The results of the regression analysis for hopelessness are summed up in Chart 7.

In the entire sample, hopelessness was in the closest correlation with the individual aspirations, explaining 21% of the variance of hopelessness. Hopelessness was in close negative interrelation with the likelihood of personal advancement and the realization of the intrinsic aspirations, and in a positive interrelation with the importance of intrinsic aspirations and wealth, as well as with the realization of social commitment. So, hopelessness may arise when an individual, while making the satisfaction of intrinsic aspirations an important goal in life, believes that these aspirations are satisfied in the present and that there is little hope to satisfy them in the future.

In an examination according to the two genders, we found that individual aspirations explained a larger proportion of their variance of hopelessness in the case of men (men: 33.4%, women: 21.8%). In addition to the importance of dissatisfied intrinsic aspirations, a lack of health at the moment may also lead to hopelessness, even if the prospects of health in the future are good. In the case of women, the emergence of a sense of hopelessness was found to be in the closest correlation with the importance of wealth, the lack of wealth in the present, and the deficit of present and future personal advancement.

Chart 8 contains the regression analysis of dissatisfaction.

Chart 8. The regression of the sense of dissatisfaction for the scales of the Aspiration Inventory (approved models; $p<0.05$)

Predictor	Béta	t	p<
Total: $F_{totál}$=38,816; df=2/712; p<0.000			
Personal advancement: probability	-0.291	-6,200	0.000
Intrinsic: importance	0.150	3,614	0.000
Women: $F_{totál}$=32,986; df=2/545; p<0.000			
Personal advancement: probability	-0.367	-8,115	0.000
Intrinsic: importance	0.136	3,004	0.000
Men: $F_{totál}$=14,755; df=1/167; p<0.000			
Personal advancement: probability	-0.291	-3,841	0.000

The results of the regression analysis of dissatisfaction suggest that in the entire sample, there is a powerful negative correlation between the sense of dissatisfaction and the likelihood of personal advancement and a positive correlation with the importance of intrinsic aspirations, together explaining 10% of the variance of dissatisfaction. A person, to whom the satisfaction of intrinsic aspirations is important, but who believes that there is little hope for personal advancement in the future, may become dissatisfied. In the case of women, a larger proportion of the variance of dissatisfaction was explained by the individual aspirations (11.2%) than in the case of men (8.4%). In both genders, the source of dissatisfaction was the deficit in the likelihood of personal advancement, to which the importance of intrinsic aspirations was coupled in the case of women.

4. Conclusion

In the course of our examinations, in both genders, there were smaller shifts of emphasis in terms of judging the importance of individual aspirations; in college students, the intrinsic aspirations were found to be more characteristic. In the case of women, the priority order was health, social relationships, and personal advancement; in the case of men, the order was personal advancement, health, and social relationships, respectively.

Out of the symptoms of depression, social withdrawal was found to be in the closest correlation with the importance of personal aspirations and, within that, the lack of intrinsic aspirations. When looking at the two genders separately from the aspect of the interrelations between depression symptoms and the importance of certain aspirations, there appeared to be a close correlation with more depression symptoms than in the case of women, indicating the lack of intrinsic aspirations. These results confirm the research findings of Kasser and Ryan [5], with the addition that the lack of intrinsic aspirations in itself may lead to the emergence of sub-clinical depression symptoms.

The specific depression symptoms were found to be in a close interrelation with the likelihood and realization of almost all of the individual aspirations. Within that, the correlation was more powerful with the intrinsic than with the extrinsic aspirations (in the case of men, a much more powerful connection was found between the depression symptoms and the likelihood and realization of almost all aspirations than in the case of women).

When examining the connections of all the three categories of individual aspirations (importance, likelihood, and realization) together with depression, we found that depression was in a close negative correlation with the likelihood of personal advancement and social relationships; and the realization of health, a positive correlation with the importance ascribed to the intrinsic aspirations, that together explain almost one quarter of the variance of depression. When the two genders are examined separately, we find a closer correlation between depression and individual aspirations in the case of men, explaining one-third of the variance.

The depression symptoms characteristic of college students (guilt, fatigue, indecisiveness, pessimism, and dissatisfaction) were in a much closer correlation with the importance, likelihood, and realization of the individual aspirations than in the case of women.

Out of the depression symptoms above, the closest correlation was found to be with hopelessness in both sexes. While in the case of men, the importance of—currently dissatisfied—intrinsic aspirations might lead to hopelessness, in the case of women the primary reason for hopelessness was the importance—and current lack—of wealth.

In the other depression symptoms, the explaining force of the interrelation with the individual aspirations was different between men and women. In the case of men, the order was fatigue, indecisiveness, guilt, and dissatisfaction; whereas in the case of women, it was guilt, dissatisfaction, indecisiveness, and fatigue, respectively. In both genders, the depression symptoms were in close correlation with one of the intrinsic aspirations.

As a summary of our research findings, we may conclude that in the case of college students, the intrinsic aspirations also serve as a protective factor in preserving health, the prevention of the emergence of sub-clinical depression symptoms, and through it, the creation and maintenance of mental balance.

REFERENCES

[1] Demetrovics ZS., & Nagy GY.(2001): Személyes törekvések és egészség. [Personal strivings and Health]. *Magyar Pszichológiai Szemle.* 56: 513-538.

[2] Kendler, H.H. (1999): The role of value in the world of psychology. *American Psychologist.* 54: 828-835.

[3] Deci, E.L., & Ryan, R.M. (2000): The "what" and "why" of goal pursuits: Human needs and the self-determination of behaviour. *Psychological Inquiry.* 11: 227-268.

[4] Kasser T. (2005): Az anyagiasság súlyos ára [The High Price of Materialism]. *Ursus Libris*, Budapest, 2005.

[5] Kasser, T., & Ryan, R.M. (1993): A dark side of the American dream: correlates of financial success as a central life aspiration. *Journal of Personality and Social Psychology.* 65: 410-422.

[6] Beck AT, & Beck RW. (1972): Screening depressed patients in family practice. A rapid technique. *Postgrad. Med.* 52: 81-85.

[7] Margitics F (2005): Prediszponáló tényezők kapcsolata a szubklinikus depressziós tünetegyüttessel főiskolai hallgatóknál [Predisposition factors and subclinical depression among healthy college students], *Psychiatria Hungarica.* 20: 211-223.

[8] Volk RJ, & Pace TM, & Parchman ML. (1993): Screening for depression in primary care patients: dimensionality of short of the Beck Depression Inventory. *Psychol. Assess.* 5: 173-181.

[9] Vredenburg K, c Kramels L, & Flett GL. (1985): Reexamining the Beck Depression Inventory: the long and short of it. *Psychol. Reports.* 56: 767-778.

[10] Margitics F. (2005): A diszfunkcionális attitűdök, megküzdési stratégiák és az attribúciós stílus összefüggése a szubklinikus depressziós tünetegyüttessel főiskolai hallgatóknál [The interrelations between subclicinal depression syndrome and disfunctional attitudes and family socialization at college students], *Mentálhigiéné és Pszichoszomatika.* 6: 95-122.

[11] Kasser, T., & Ryan, R.M. (1996), Further examining the American dream: differential correlates of intrinsic and extrinsic goals. *Personality and Social Psychology Bulletin. 22,* 280-287.

[12] Csorba, J., & Dinya, E., & Párt, S., & Solymos, J., (1994): Életesemény kutatás és serdülőkor. A középiskolás életesemény kérdőív bemutatása. [Life event research and adolescence. The Hungarian version of the Junior High Life Experiences Survey.] *Magyar Pszichológiai Szemle. 50,* 67-83.

[13] Deci, E.L., & Ryan, R.M. (1985): Intrinsic Motivation and Self-determination in *Human Behavior.* Plenum, New York.

[14] Kasser, T., & Ryan, R.M. (1996): Further examining the American dream: differential correlates of intrinsic and extrinsic goals. *Personality and Social Psychology Bulletin.* 22: 280-287.

[15] V. Komlósi, A., & Rózsa S., & Bérdi M., & Móricz É., & Horváth D. (2006). Az Aspirációs Index hazai alkalmazásával szerzett tapasztalatok. [Experiences obtained with the domestic application of the Aspiration Index.] *Magyar Pszichológiai Szemle. 61,* 237-250.

[16] Szondy M. (2004): A szubjektív jóllét és a törekvések kapcsolata késői serdülőkorban [The connection between subjective well-being and aspirations durig late adolescence]. *Alkalmazott Pszichológia.* 2004. 4: 53-72.

[17] Margitics F. (2006): *Depresszió. (Depression)* Krúdy Könyvkiadó, Nyíregyháza.

INDEX

A

achievement, 4
activation, 2
adaptation, 8, 10
adolescence, 56
adolescents, 10, 13, 14, 20, 21
age, 5, 6, 11, 13, 14, 33, 40
anorexia, 41
anxiety, 3, 40
appetite, 46
application, 35, 56
aspiration, x, xi, 2, 13, 14, 18, 35, 37, 55
attitudes, 16, 56
attribution, 5
authority, 4
autonomy, 9, 39

B

basic needs, 9
Beck Depression Inventory (BDI), 44, 45, 48, 49, 56
behavior, ix, 4, 38, 39
bottom-up, 3
breakdown, x, 1, 10, 25, 42, 47, 51

C

classes, 5
clinical depression, 40, 54, 55
college students, ix, x, 1, 5, 10, 13, 32, 33, 37, 40, 42, 43, 50, 54, 55, 56
community, 40
competence, 39
compliance, 10, 32, 33
components, 3, 6, 7, 8, 41
concentrates, 39
consent, 6, 40
control, 4
correlation, x, xi, 2, 6, 20, 21, 27, 28, 29, 30, 31, 32, 33, 34, 37, 44, 46, 47, 49, 50, 51, 53, 54, 55

D

decisions, 4, 42, 44, 51, 52
definition, x, 2, 37
depressed, 56
depression, ix, x, 3, 37, 38, 40, 41, 42, 43, 44, 45, 46, 47, 48, 49, 50, 54, 55, 56
deviation, x, 2, 13, 14
dimensionality, 56
dispersion, 10, 13
dissatisfaction, xi, 38, 41, 42, 43, 46, 50, 53, 55

dream, 35, 55, 56

E

emotional well-being, 4
emotions, 2, 3
energy, 8
estimating, xi, 37
examinations, 54
extraversion, 4
extrinsic motivation, 10

F

failure, 41, 45, 47, 48
fairness, 35
family, 7, 56
fatigue, xi, 38, 42, 46, 51, 55
fear, 3, 41
feelings, 39, 40
females, x, 37, 42
fulfillment, 2

G

gender, x, 2, 5, 34, 40, 46, 47
goals, ix, 4, 5, 6, 9, 13, 26, 33, 35, 38, 39, 56
groups, 2, 6, 14, 15, 16, 17, 18, 19
growth, xi, 9, 13, 14, 32, 33, 38
guilt, 41, 42, 43, 55

H

happiness, 3, 34
harm, 32
harmony, 32
health, ix, xi, 1, 5, 10, 13, 14, 16, 20, 21, 25, 31, 32, 33, 34, 37, 38, 39, 40, 44, 46, 47, 49, 51, 53, 54, 55
health psychology, vi, ix, 38
hopelessness, xi, 38, 44, 46, 52, 53, 55
human, ix, 4, 8, 21, 25, 26, 27, 28, 29, 33, 36, 38, 39
human behavior, 4
human values, 39
hypothesis, 32, 33, 34

I

id, 16
idiographic approach, 35
implementation, x, 2
indecisiveness, 41, 43, 52, 55
indicators, ix, 1, 5, 6, 10, 16, 18, 20, 21, 22, 23, 24, 25, 26, 30, 33, 34
inner tension, 8
inspiration, 4
integration, 9
internal value, 39
interrelations, 4, 47, 51, 54, 56
intimacy, 39
intrinsic, x, xi, 1, 5, 6, 9, 10, 13, 14, 15, 16, 18, 19, 20, 21, 25, 26, 29, 30, 32, 33, 34, 35, 37, 39, 40, 44, 46, 47, 49, 51, 53, 54, 55, 56
intrinsic motivation, 10
intrinsic value, 39, 40
inventories, 6

J

judge, 9
judgment, 3, 39

L

life satisfaction, 16, 21, 25, 33
Life Satisfaction Scale, 7, 10, 14, 15, 19
lifespan, 35
lifestyle, 18
likelihood, x, 2, 6, 9, 19, 20, 21, 23, 25, 26, 27, 28, 29, 30, 31, 33, 34, 44, 45, 46, 49, 50, 51, 53, 54, 55
Likert scale, 8
linear, 25, 49, 50

linear regression, 25, 49, 50
longitudinal study, 35

M

maintenance, 55
males, x, 37
market, 35
marriage, 3, 7
measures, 7
median, 6, 40
men, ix, xi, 1, 4, 5, 6, 11, 13, 14, 26, 27, 28, 29, 30, 31, 32, 33, 34, 37, 40, 42, 44, 46, 47, 49, 50, 51, 52, 53, 54, 55
mental development, 39
mental health, x, 34, 37
mental state, 39
models, 2, 25, 26, 28, 29, 30, 31, 39, 49, 50, 51, 52, 53
money, 4, 39
mood, 6, 7, 8, 10, 11, 16, 18, 20, 21, 22, 23, 24, 29, 30, 33, 39, 40
motivation, 4, 9
motives, 9

N

narcissism, 40
negative emotions, 3
negative life events, 41, 42
negative relation, 47
neuroticism, 4

O

openness, 39
organic, ix, 38
orientation, 40

P

partnership, 52
patients, 56
perceptions, ix, 38
personal goals, ix, 4, 38
personal problems, x, 2, 7, 8, 10, 18, 19, 20, 21, 25, 30, 31, 33, 34
personal relations, x, 2, 16, 27, 32, 34, 50
personal relationship, 16, 50
personality, ix, 2, 3, 4, 5, 9, 34, 35, 38, 39
pessimism, 41, 42, 43, 55
philosophers, 2
play, x, 37, 38
pleasure, 3, 7, 16, 17, 21, 28, 29, 33, 39
positive correlation, xi, 4, 6, 21, 25, 26, 33, 38, 44, 49, 51, 53, 54
positive emotions, 3, 40
positive relation, 9, 21, 33, 50
positive relationship, 33, 50
power, xi, 38
predictors, 25, 49
pressure, 39
prevention, 55
primary care, 56
probability, x, xi, 1, 12, 14, 21, 25, 26, 28, 29, 30, 31, 37, 47, 49, 50, 51, 52, 53
protective factors, ix, x, 37
protective role, 38
psychological variables, 39
psychology, ix, 4, 38, 55
punishment, 41, 45, 46, 47, 48

Q

questionnaire, 8, 9, 10, 41, 42

R

regression, 25, 26, 27, 28, 29, 30, 31, 49, 50, 51, 52, 53
regression analysis, 25, 26, 27, 28, 29, 30, 31, 49, 50, 51, 53
relationship, x, 2, 21, 33, 34, 46, 47, 50
relationships, xi, 12, 16, 22, 23, 24, 25, 26, 28, 37, 44, 45, 48, 49, 50, 52, 54
reliability, 8, 10
representative samples, 5

reputation, 10, 13, 14, 16, 32, 33
reservation, xi, 37
resources, 4
risk, 50

S

sadness, 3, 8, 41, 47
sample, 6, 7, 10, 11, 13, 14, 15, 25, 26, 27, 28, 29, 30, 31, 32, 33, 35, 42, 43, 44, 46, 47, 49, 51, 53
satisfaction, 3, 4, 6, 7, 8, 10, 16, 18, 19, 20, 21, 25, 26, 33, 39, 40, 53
scarcity, 3
scores, x, 1, 6, 7, 10, 15, 44
self-determination theory, 9, 39
self-esteem, x, 2, 7, 8, 10, 16, 17, 21, 27, 28, 33, 34, 39
self-expression, 2
self-image, 41
skills, 4
social behavior, 40
social environment, 8
social relations, x, xi, 1, 5, 10, 13, 14, 15, 16, 20, 32, 33, 37, 39, 44, 46, 49, 54
social relationships, xi, 37, 44, 49, 54
social responsibility, 13, 14, 15, 16, 18, 20, 33
social skills, 4
social withdrawal, 41, 43, 44, 46, 54
socialization, 56
somatic complaints, 20
somatic symptoms, ix, 1, 7, 8, 10, 11, 18, 19, 20, 21, 25, 31, 32, 34
spiritual, 39
sports, 4
standard deviation, 6, 13, 40, 42
statistical analysis, 11, 13, 42
statistics, 10, 11, 12, 13, 42
students, ix, x, 1, 5, 6, 7, 10, 13, 15, 19, 20, 32, 33, 35, 37, 40, 42, 43, 50, 54, 55, 56
subjective, ix, 1, 2, 3, 4, 5, 6, 7, 8, 20, 21, 22, 23, 24, 25, 32, 33, 34, 35, 38, 39, 56
subjective well-being, ix, 1, 2, 3, 4, 5, 6, 7, 8, 20, 21, 22, 23, 24, 25, 32, 33, 34, 35, 38, 39, 56
suffering, 18
suicide, 41, 42, 43
susceptibility, 49
symptom, 42
symptoms, ix, xi, 1, 6, 7, 8, 10, 11, 18, 19, 20, 21, 22, 23, 24, 25, 31, 32, 33, 34, 37, 38, 40, 42, 43, 44, 45, 46, 47, 48, 50, 54, 55
syndrome, 56

T

tension, 39
time, 31, 32, 50

U

uncertainty, 39

V

validity, 7
values, ix, 1, 5, 10, 13, 14, 15, 38, 39, 40
variables, 40, 50
variance, x, 2, 4, 25, 26, 27, 28, 29, 30, 31, 32, 34, 49, 50, 51, 53, 54

W

wealth, x, xi, 1, 5, 10, 13, 14, 16, 20, 21, 25, 27, 32, 33, 38, 39, 44, 46, 47, 53, 55
well-being, ix, 1, 2, 3, 4, 5, 6, 7, 8, 20, 21, 22, 23, 24, 25, 32, 33, 34, 35, 38, 39, 56
withdrawal, 8, 45, 46, 48
women, ix, xi, 1, 4, 5, 6, 11, 13, 14, 26, 27, 29, 30, 31, 32, 33, 37, 40, 44, 46, 47, 49, 50, 51, 52, 53, 54, 55